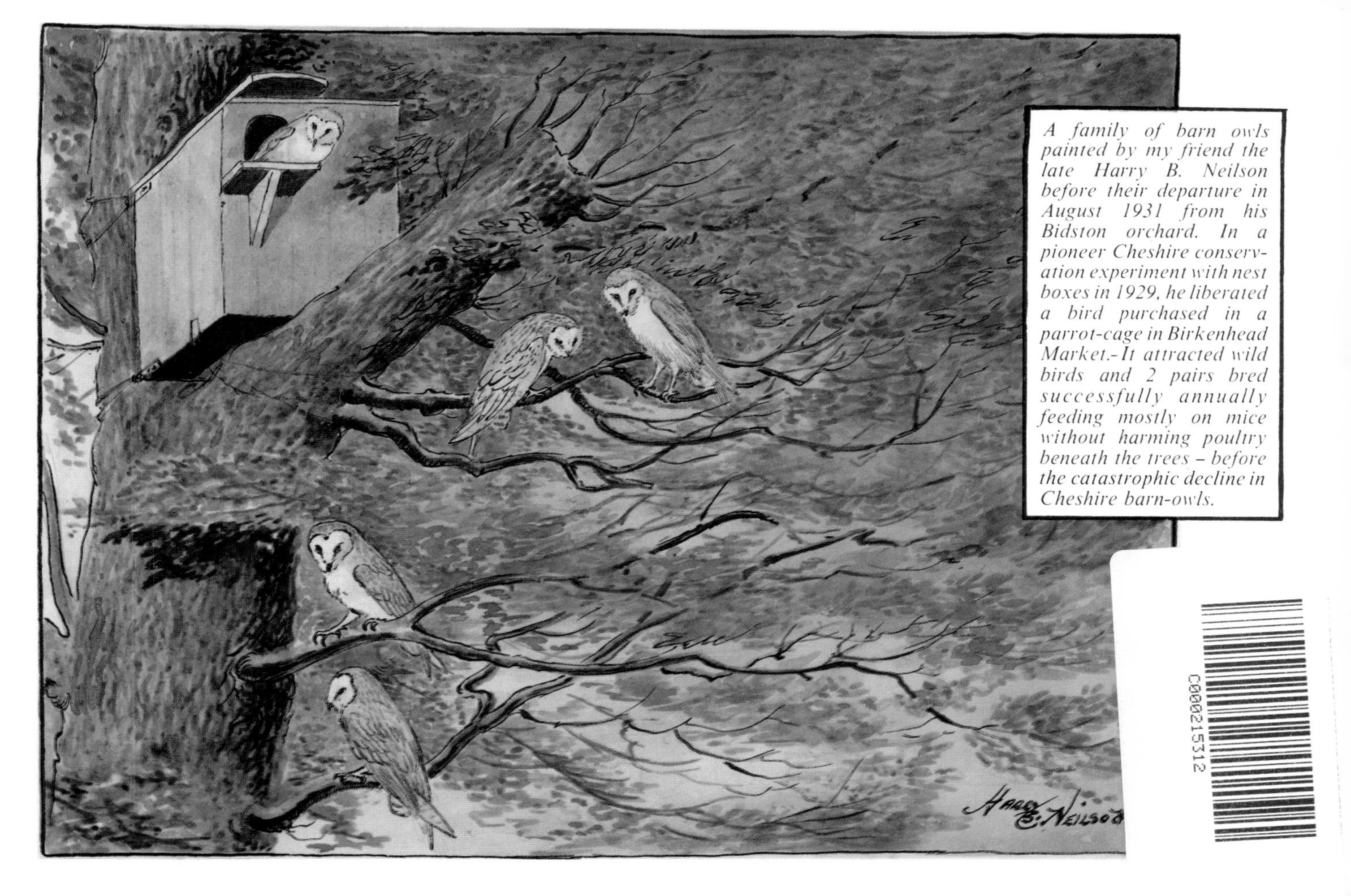

A family of barn owls painted by my friend the late Harry B. Neilson before their departure in August 1931 from his Bidston orchard. In a pioneer Cheshire conservation experiment with nest boxes in 1929, he liberated a bird purchased in a parrot-cage in Birkenhead Market.- It attracted wild birds and 2 pairs bred successfully annually feeding mostly on mice without harming poultry beneath the trees – before the catastrophic decline in Cheshire barn-owls.

Front Cover (designed by Eric R. Monks)
Ringed Plover, a Cheshire nesting bird and inland passage migrant.

First published 1988 by Countyvise Limited, 1 & 3 Grove Road, Rock Ferry, Birkenhead, Wirral L42 3XS.

Photoset and printed by Birkenhead Press Limited, 1 & 3 Grove Road, Rock Ferry, Birkenhead, Merseyside L42 3XS.

ISBN 0 907768 08 3

Bird-Watching in Cheshire

by

Eric Hardy

Contents

Owing to unavoidable delay since this manuscript was completed, the following brief update is appended:

BIDSTON WD, Firecrest song Apr/87, Iceland gull, Dock Overflow Feb/88; BURWARDSLEY, Nightjar June/86; DEE ESTY, record 10,000 Redshank Oct/87, 5,200 Heswall; Steelworks Reserve up to 28 Cormorants late Aug, 4 Goldeneye winter, Little Ringed Plover, Wheatear n/87, 280 Common Tern fledged raft, 20 new "island"/87, Denhall Pools, Wilson's Phalarope Sept/87, 15 Twite Feb/87; Eccleston-Eaton, 25 feral Mandarin Dec/87; Eaton-Aldford. n. Mandarin; Eaton Pk, 75 nests Heronry; EAST, Brown Knowle, n Pied Flycatcher; FIDDLERS FERRY, 64 Sand-Martin n/87, 230 Shoveler v. Oct/87; FRODSHAM MARSH/WEAVER, Osprey Apr, Richard's Pipit May/87, Broad-billed Sandpiper May/86, Baird's Sept/85, Semi-palmated, Oct/82, Mediterranean Gull Sept, Little Gulls; Shoveler n/87; HALE DECOY, 590 Mallard Sept/87, 2 Garganey, Ramsbrook Apr/87, Record Mersey flock 146 Gt Black-backed Gulls, Mersey Feb/88, 11 Twite, to Oglet, Jan/87; HOYLAKE RED ROCKS, Ring-billed Gull, Jan/86; HILBRE, Cory's Shearwater Sept/86; 1,000 Grey Plover, tide, Mar/88; MERSEY, INCE GORSE 16 Twite Feb/87; LEASOWE Breakwater Isles, 600 Turnstones, 900 Redshank, tide Mar/88, 310 Ringed Plover Oct/87; Macclesfield Forest, Crossbills Aug/87; Manisty 33 Herons Nov/87, Grey Crow; MARBURY (GT BUDWORTH) MERE, Bittern Feb/87; MORETON 'QUARRY' Railway Flash, Ruddy Duck, Goosander, Mediterranean Gull Nov, 5 Scaup Dec/87; development plans may disturb with boating; PICKMERE, 17 Scaup Nov/87; RISLEY MOSS, Goshawk Feb/88; ROSTHERNE MERE, 48/100 Kittiwakes March passage/87 and previous; 3,500 Pochard Feb/88, Red Kite Nov/86, Franklin's gull May, 75 Gadwall No/87; RUNCORN, Guillemot gales Dec/88, Little Ringed Plover n. docks/87; SANDBACH FLASHES, American Wigeon, Green-winged Teal, Water-Pipit, 2 Peregrines Nov/87 etc.; SHOTWICK LAKE, Red and Black-throated Divers, Slavonian and Black-necked Grebes, Hobby, Little Gull, Mediterranean Gull Nov/87, Little Crake Apr, Garganey, Smew, Yellow-legged Herring-Gull Oct/Dec, Glaucous Gull, Osprey Sept/87; STANLOW, Lapland Buntings Oct/87; TABLEY, 37 Herons/87; TATTON, Little Gull Aug, Mandarins, n. Wood Warbler; TEG'S NOSE, n. Wood Warbler; THORTON MANOR, Goldeneye Dec; WALLASEY, Woodcock, Magazine Lane, Dec, Tawny Owls, Rake Lane; WEAVER ESTY, Mediterranean Gull July, 4,000 Dunlin Nov/87; WILDBOARCLOUGH, Hen-Harrier March; WINSFORD FLASH, Kittiwakes and Scaup Mar/88; WOOLSTON, Hobby July, 3,000 Teal Nov, 23 Russian Whitefronted Geese Dec/87, Honey-Buzzard May/86, Laughing Gull Nov/85, Water-Pipit; n Black-necked Grebe, Kingfisher/87.

BARN-OWL: 8 ringed, released mid-Wirral/86, n Thurstaston. 1 killed Bidston Motorway Flyover/88 where food-pellets I examined all skulls and bones field-voles, no birds or rats. Hunting nr A55 roundabout, Chester. Hawk Trust Report 83/84 Census, 13 pr Cheshire, 86% decline from 239 pairs when I conducted 1932 RSPB census here. COLLARED DOVE. None n Stanlow-Manisty thickets 1988, Woodpigeons recovered former nesting domination.

Foreword

With spring or winter in the air and hardly a bird allowed to fly past unrecorded, a county which offers Northwest Europe's greatest concentrations of pintail and teal, some of Britain's biggest flocks of shelduck, oystercatchers and knot, and largest populations of heron and great crested grebe luring bird-watchers from all over the country, packing Parkgate, Hilbre, the Weaver estuary and the Sunday morning hide at Rostherne's great mere where one never met another bird-watcher unless by arrangement before the war, merits attention.

There's no shortage of Field Guides to identify birds. Finding them is the problem. Supplemented by Ordnance Survey maps, this is a guide to the best places for seeing them within the old county boundary (Watsonian Vice-County 58 in scientific recording) according to tide, wind and season. It is developed from study courses on Cheshire birds I began at Burton Manor Adult County College in the 1950s and 60s, and over half-a-century's field-work.

Cheshire bird-laws are like anywhere else. Nobody has legal ownership of wild birds or exclusive rights to watch them, though laws protect birds and their haunts.

Cheshire ornithology has progressed from collecting to conservation, from shooting museum "skins" or listing birds to improving habitats for nesting (like Woolston), feeding (wigeon on Ince Bank) and roosting (Parkgate marshes); from finding rarities before reading their obituary notices (Tarporley churchwardens paid 5p in 1664 for shooting kites) to studying migration by mist-netting (from Woolston to Bidston, Thurstaston and the Dee marshes), colour-marking, censusing populations of estuarine waders and waterfowl on the meres. and mapping distribution. Knowledge is not a closed book for the privileged few at the end of a telephoned grape-vine. I have shared information through my weekly "Countryside" feature in Liverpool Daily Post for over 60 years and my twice weekly "Countryside" programme broadcast almost since the inception of BBC Radio Merseyside. I have lectured to Cheshire ornithological societies at Knutsford, Sandbach, Nantwich, Wilmslow, Lymm, Runcorn, Mid-Cheshire, Chester, Hale, etc., and defended Cheshire heronries and Mersey marshes at public enquiries. From 1932, I represented naturalists on the committee of the Associated Learned Societies of Liverpool & District and formed the ornithological section in the now defunct Liverpool Field Club and in 1938 formed the Merseyside Naturalists' Association. I was an active member of Lancashire & Cheshire Fauna Committee before any Cheshire member since the late A.W. Boyd.

I wrote this book too old for social-climbing ambitions. After watching birds over most of Britain, I appreciate where Cheshire offers more than most places and that their future lies in preserving their habitats. There must no longer be a "closed shop" in bird-watching. All who do not harm birds have equal right in law to watch, study and conserve them. As I once remarked in a lecture to Manchester Ornithological Society, if I trod on anyone's toes it was because they were deliberately placed in one's way. Many active ornithologists do not report their records to the national rarities committee or local Reports. Cheshire lists have never been complete, through lack of liaison until quite recently. May this book meet your needs with an awareness of ecology as well as new birds for your life-list — our need for the tonic of silence on Mersey and Dee broken only by nostalgic cries of curlew or the snipe in startled flight; our need to smell only the tang of incoming tide and be refreshed by its gleam ahead. My thanks to so many friends who shared their discoveries, or allowed me to use their photogtraphs, to landowners who permit me on private property and to my publishers for their help with this work.

Abbreviations

ad: adult; c/3 clutch of 3 eggs; CTC: Cheshire Trust for Conservation; HW: high water; LW: low water; MNA: Merseyside Naturalists' Association; ML: marine lake; MRG: Merseyside Ringing Group; NT: National Trust; n: nests; NCC: Nature Conservancy Council; p.m.: passage-migrant; P.M.: post mortem; q.v.: which see; r: ringed; res: reserve; resvr: reservoir; RSPB: Royal Society for Protection of Birds; SF: sewage-farm; SW: sewage-works; sp: species, spp: plural; SQ: sand-quarry; sv: summer visitor; v: visitors; wv: winter visitor; y: young; *nationally outstanding bird-haunt. CCT now CTC.

Our Study Area

Birds are less county-minded than their recorders. You may search the sky from Hilbre to Meols, Leasowe and New Brighton when westerly autumn gales, tearing across Liverpool Bay, lash the coastline with raging surf, and see marine shearwaters, petrels, auks, skuas, phalaropes, arctic gulls and once an albatross brought to us from their migration through the eastern Irish Sea. Half the wild wateriness where Dee flocks of over 90,000 waders pattern the sky or seek a green refuge on its marshes beyond Burton (watched most conveniently from Cheshire) belongs to Wales. East Cheshire's black-walled upthrusting sweep of sheep-grazed moorland hiils where dark stone walls stitch together miles of windy heath and heather, borrowed its wild, upland glory from the Derbyshire and Staffordshire Peak, rising to 1,900 ft Bleak Hill above Featherbed Moss on the Yorkshire border. Over 40 miles wide, south Cheshire's central plain with reed-girt, grebe-haunted meres, drained by the wooded valley of the River Weaver winding its way 45 miles from Peckforton Hills to the Staffordshire border then back to its grave in the Manchester Ship Canal, is part of the north Shropshire plain.

Shaped like a bird's wing or a chicken with its head in Featherbed Moss, with Macclesfield Forest in its crop, and the Wirral peninsula for a tail Cheshire lacks Lancashire's productive sanddunes (now levelled and drained for golf) and its flat mossland goose-fields. Nine-tenths of the county is Triassic new red sandstone. Its central sand-quarries like Sandiway, Chelford, Arclid, Acre Nook and Shakerley are the haunt of sand-martins and their pools of little ringed plovers. Overlaid with boulder-clay, it is the winter haunt of golden plover and lapwings where one loses one's wellies in the wet fields, but with house-sparrows nesting in the cracks of England's highest clay cliffs at Thurstaston shore. Brine-pumping from the Keuper saltbeds produced wader-haunted subsidence-flashes at Sandbach and Northwich, and in one's own time Tatton Park's Melchett duck-pool. Meres may be shallow glistening subsidences like Tatton, artificially dammed like Tabley or gouged deep by glaciers like Rostherne. East and Northeast rises the wildly beautiful gritstone of the Cheshire Pennines.

Convergence of tidal streams from Anglesey and the North Channel bring the rewarding virtue of the coast, an 8 metre range at mean spring tides with a vast intertidal feeding zone luring some of Britain's biggest flocks of knot, oystercatcher, godwits, sanderling, curlew, dunlin, grey plover and redshank; and exposing estuarine and offshore tidal banks.

One of the driest areas on the west coast of Britain, mild 119 square mile Wirral peninsula, highest at 340 ft Heswall Hill, has about half

Manisty Bay Reserve, from Stanlow Point (lower) to Mount Manisty (upper), Britain's major estuarine haunt of pintail and teal.
(Photo courtesy Manchester Ship Canal Coy).

the rainfall of Southport and a quarter that of western Lakeland. Its coast is exposed to winds between WNE and N with a full fetch of 10 miles to howl across the Irish Sea and fling upon our shores in September or October grey phalarope, Leach's and storm petrels, pomerine, great and arctic skuas, Manx, sooty and Balearic shearwaters, Sabine's gulls and once an albatross. In the rain-shadow of the purple mountain-line of Wales, Deeside has even less rain and is outside the usual zone of severe thunderstorms which spread north from France. October and August average wettest, April and March driest. The estuaries keep Wirral mild and winter becomes colder to the east. In the big frost of January 1963 I noted the Mersey fell to minus 1 deg C at the surface and -0.8 deg at the bottom. It is the wintering haunt of reed-buntings, greenfinches, herons, etc, ringed in colder eastern and midland counties and the continent. Its coastal west is poor in woodland, hence fewer chaffinches. Conservationists fight a losing battle to save its 3,000 field-ponds from pollution where Mersey and Dee wild duck flight to feed at night.

Except for sandstone Hilbre with its purple sandpipers and turnstones, Hoylake's Hilbre Point ("Red Rocks") and New Brighton's Perch Rock, there is little rocky shore. Two sandy estuaries of Mersey and Dee widen into marshes with miles of flat mud-banks stretching all around one, ideal for godwits, greenshank, curlew and spotted redshank; or overgrown with Atriplex, Halimone, Spartina and Aster, providing cover for water-rails and rodents which attract short-eared owls and long-winged harriers. Hoylake Red Rocks golf-corner has one of the best land falls of rarer passerine migrants; Mersey and Dee the biggest wildfowl and wader-flocks at high water; Weaver Bend and Sandbach Flashes the best inland waders; Rostherne and Doddington meres the best inland duck. Manchester Ship Canal protects the Mersey flocks from dogs and disturbance birds meet on the Dee.

Wooded sandstone ridges rise above the central plain from Overton and Frodsham Castle Park with wood-warblers, Helsby (once a hoopoe), and Upper Burwardsley-Peckforton-Bickerton (with pied flycatchers). From Alderley Edge gritstone rises 1,600-1,900 ft to Cheshire's highest hills in the East, Bleak Hill, Shining Tor and 1,659 ft Shutlin's Low (978 695) with typical moorland twite, ring-ouzel,dipper, redstart and wheatear though much of the Goyt grouse-moors went to Derbyshire in the 1972 Local Government Act. A few dunlin nest in moors near Macclesfield, Lamaload, Longdendale.

Cheshire is rich in walled parks where squires took possession of the landscape, some public like Tatton, Arrowe, Dunham, Lyme, Marbury and in part Cholmondeley with deciduous woods, heronries and waterfowl-lakes. Combermere (private) has the largest lake in English parks. The Dee valley links migrating birds from the Severn, like cormorants. The Mersey is a route for wigeon and shelduck across the Yorkshire-Derbyshire Pennines.

Stanlow Point, low tide, a Mersey bird-reserve.
(Photo R. Lakin, courtesy Manchester Ship Canal Coy.)

It is possible to see 100 species in a day if one races around as varied haunts as possible in a fast car from dawn to dusk, over 200 in a year; but most people seek more leisurely bird-watching. Having pioneered watching and recording prewar Frodsham sludge-beds, the Weaver estuary and Stanlow Point, organised the first bird-watchers' field-meetings there and at Hilbre, the first seabird survey of Leach's petrels from ships in the Rock Channel, the first bird-population counts, and negotiated reserves at the former 1942 Moreton brickworks flash and postwar Weston Marsh, Stanlow and Dee steelworks' pools, I have seen great changes in bird-watching techniques and opportunities here. Since MNA published the first inch-to-the-mile wall-map of Liverpool Area bird-distribution in 1942, much has been lost to building over North Wirral, drainage of Frodsham, Aldford and Puddington marshes, industrial tipping and tree-felling. We gained Shotwick Lake on the Welsh border and 14 new reserves. Shooting pressure has been reduced on Mersey and Dee where bittern, grey phalarope and peregrine were shot openly and many former egg and skin-collecting critics of me as a "protectionist" obtained remunerative posts in conservation bodies. When I was the R.S.P.B.'s voluntary local lecturer over half-a-century ago it had barely a score of members where now I have lectured to five times as many at its North Cheshire and Wirral branches, and it has 7,600 in the county. There are 20 other bird societies apart from falconers, fowlers and aviculturalists. Liason and co-ordination improved more slowly from appalling bias and incompleteness in Cheshire recording. It is necessary to withhold some locations of rarities for conservation. The telephoned grape-vine brought over 50 bird-watchers tramping-out lapwing-nests to see Frodsham's stilt-sandpiper before any newspaper or radio notice. Liaison means sitting around a table as equals, not a take-over bid. Problems of privileged bird-watching, aggressive recording or ambitious new associations can only be met with a code of goodwill, not a "closed shop."

In 1963 I had a working lunch with directors of the old Dee steelworks, to form the first bird-reserve on its marshes. In 1972, I had a working lunch with Peter Scott and directors of C.E.G.B. at Fiddlers Ferry Power-Station, resulting in its bird-reserve — the 6th now by the Mersey — a major haunt of diving duck, saved from shooting. Conservation is no longer a dirty word; yet before the war nobody would listen to my pleas to preserve Hale Duck Decoy, and shortly after it I was "sacked" from Shooting Times for criticising the killing of scheduled birds on the Dee estuary.

Cheshire Bird-Haunts

Bird-watching is an infliction appeased by rising before dawn and racing off to meet a new bird, the wild goose's vice of getting up early. Some haunts are private. Many depend upon the right tide, wind or season if one is not to be disappointed. Most rewarding are autumn and spring wader-migrations from the wide tidal Dee mouth below West Kirby to the Weaver Estuary and the flashes, and winter's internationally qualifying wild wildfowl flocks in the contrasting yet often complementary Mersey and Dee estuaries, not pinioned cripples in a duck-zoo.

Teal and pintail, rising in Manisty Bay Gutter, Jan. 87.(Photo. Eric Hardy)

Tide-times are earlier seawards, later upriver with the best coastal bird-watching at 10 metres, especially in autumn with strong onshore winds. Strong S and W winds with a low barometer make tides higher and a little earlier than the tables, and *vice versa* with strong easterlies which drift continental hoopoes, black terns and more stints and curlew-sandpipers to inland haunts. In persistant westerlies one slips an American Field Guide into the rucksack for several newcomers from across the North Atlantic have been added to the modern list. Never wade into a rising tide and beware of high banks hiding gutters growing faster, wider and deeper in what looks like continuous sand or green salting, like ill-fated Mary who went against a rising tide to call the cattle home across the sands of Dee.

There isn't space to repeat every common migrant or nester where their absence would be more noteworthy; or accidental stragglers to chance places, like eager-eyed shrikes on the top of tall bushes and wind-drifted hoopoes barred like a Birkenhead Park rugby-player, seabirds like gannets blown anywhere inland; or to give complete lists for major haunts.

One goes to the Weaver or Sandbach for the best inland waders in autumn; to Rostherne's deep mere, the last to freeze in hard winters for the best inland duck; over to the sea-swept Wirral coast when gales howl across the Irish Sea or Neston shore where its cormorants roost in shelter. Delamere's dark pine-forest is the best bet for crossbills or siskins and winter's dusk means Parkgate car park overlooking the harriers' winter roost.

Bird-populations are always changing with alterations to their food supply and environment. As the polluted Mersey is re-oxygenated in plans for a cleaner future, invertebrate animals in the mud will alter and increase the food-chains which regulate the waders there. Temporary haunts of scavanging gulls come and go with rubbish-tips. Rooks will continue to decline with increasing urbanisation, especially in Wirral. Sludge at Frodsham Marsh and New Ferry had a long, but limited bird-attraction. The yelping chorus of wild pinkfoot and white-fronted geese is increased by hard winters; the flash of the kingfisher and the wide wings of a flying heron by successive mild seasons.

The oystercatcher, first found nesting in Cheshire at Mount Manisty, still nests on Mersey and Dee shores.

(Photo C.F. Mayos)

Since earlier histories of Cheshire birds were published, there has been a notable increase of Mediterranean, little, glaucous, ring-billed, Sabine's and Iceland gulls, pintail, teal, pinkfoot geese, collared doves, ruddy duck, sparrowhawks, peregrines and little ringed plover. Better bird-watching books helped reveal more regular visits of twite, water-pipits, black tern and many waders.Correspondingly we shared a wide decline in nightjars, turtle-doves, green woodpeckers, scoter, red-backed shrike and cirl-bunting. Black and red grouse are also fewer. Drainage ruined former snipe-bogs. Tree-felling affected heronries and rookeries.

Pintail, Teal and Wigeon in Manisty Bay Gutter, Jan. 87.(Photo. Eric Hardy)

Masses of wildfowl and waders will arrive on the Mersey from northern Europe with nowhere to go and its international status for five species lost unless we protect their habitat from barrages and reclamation of banks. More heronries will be lost unless we prevent tree-fellings, as replanting is little use in our lifetime. Stanlow, Woolston and Gayton reserves have shown how duck increase in numbers and approachability when shooting is ended. Shooting is more disturbing than bird-watching. Birds live much longer when they are not shot. "Putting back" duck-breeding policies of fowlers often brought an imbalance of common mallard, breeding earlier than usual, and a farm-like cackling of sedentary greylag geese. Long life-lists are of little consequence without recording ecological changes which influenced them. Cheshire's avi-fauna suffers an alien intrusion of escaped pet geese and exotic waterfowl from private, hybrid-breeding "duck-brothels", aviary serins, choughs, etc, zoo-flamingos and falconry's escaped lanners and goshawks whose list-swelling additions serve no scientific purpose. Conservationists should combine for birds to be conserved, regardless of who does it and without the one-sided information of fund-raising propaganda.

"Twitching" or list-ticking at least sharpens the skill of identifying difficult birds in the field, providing it does not introduce competitive rivalries or deliberate faking of records. Once you have got beyond the bird-listing stage in ornithology and your eyes no longer pop out of your binoculars at each new "tick", your interest broadens to migration and bird-behaviour, as well as conservation. Intensive sheep-grazing will reduce heather and red and black grouse on the eastern hills. Uncontrolled boating, shooting and tipping threaten many bird-haunts; but there are too many overlapping, competitive conservation bodies which lost us Leasowe sandhills and embankment pool, Burton Paddock wood-lake and Denna Hall rookery. There's a new song to be sung in your life, somewhere, some day in Cheshire, a new bird to add to your life-list, some weary-winged migrant from a foreign land, if we anticipate their arrival by preserving a suitable habitat. As small-scale maps are inadequate, it is assumed that readers will use the Ordnance Survey's, or larger, for finding our places from their map-references which follow their names here.

*Denotes nationally important.

Abbots Moss: 587689; by A49, 1 mile S of Oakmere traffic lights; 2 floating bogs, heath, limited access. n tree-pipit, grasshopper-warbler, formerly nightjar, tufted duck (before 1914), little ringed plover. Hog Lane sand-pits, v short-eared owl, and goshawk.

Adswood. Micker Brook, Cheadle, 880872. n coot. v green sandpiper, water-rail, spotted crake, little grebe, little bunting Apr-May 1983, Lapland Nov/83, rock and tree-pipits, grasshopper-warbler. Rubbish-tip.

Alderley Edge Country Park. 219 acres wooded ridge off A34 & near Wizard Café, B5087; NT; 860775. n tree-pipit, redstart, redpoll, tree-creeper, garden-warbler, green woodpecker, etc. v pied flycatcher, hobby. People pressure. See Radnor. Pied flycatchers have also nested. Warden. Nether Alderley Moat attracts winter duck.

Aldford. See Chester.

Allostock SQ. See Northwich.

Altrincham SF. West Timperley Stn, Broadheath-Brookside Farm, 903765. A classic site declined since mechanisation. Occasional dunlin, ruff, Aug-Sept, shoveler, stone-curlew Aug/48, little stint, wood and green sandpipers, water-rail, greenshank, white wagtail, pied wagtail roost, red-rumped swallow July/63, corn-bunting. Old records lesser yellowlegs and marsh-sandpiper show what passes through the area. Nearby Carrington Moss, 745915, and Brookheys Covert: corn-bunting, willow-tit, v turtle dove, golden plover, Savis warbler Apr/81.

Arclid SQ. 778624. Sand-martin; tufted duck, kingfisher, rookery.

Appleton (Walton Hall) Resvr. Warrington, 602843. n great crested and little grebes, ruddy duck, occasional little ringed plover. Sometimes drains low in summer; angling disturbance. v. duck, up to 125 pochard, goldeneye, occasional goosander, green and wood-sandpipers, spotted redshank, red-necked phalarope, marsh-harrier, black tern.

Arrowe Park. See Birkenhead. Astle, see Chelford.

Ashley Wood. Birkenheath Lane, Tatton. 761836. Wood-side fence bird-feeders, lane-end stop for cars. 5 titmice, nuthatch, sparrowhawk, etc. Fields: golden plover flock, curlew has n.

Astbury SQ. 848615. Sand-martin.

Immature Iceland gull photographed on Parkgate shore by John Edelsten, February 1954.

Astmoor Marsh. Part-tidal, Runcorn; footpath via Ship Canal Old Quay Bridge 832520. Up to 2,000 winter mallard, 500 teal, pintail, wigeon, pochard, shoveler, shelduck, sand-martin flocks, water-rail, former little ringed plover n old sewage-beds 1984, with snipe, sedge warbler, redshank (Norton Marsh) v herons, p.m. snow-bunting, Temminck's stint Aug/73.

Bache House. Private. See Hurleston, n. tufted duck, v 6 green sandpipers July/85, kingfisher, water-rail.

Baddiley Mere. 593503 v teal, wigeon, etc. Shoveler n 1932, ruddy and tufted duck, little grebe, Canada goose, willow-tit. v little ringed plover and waders in droughts. Also nesting great crested grebe, marshtit, tufted and ruddy dick, lesser spotted woodpecker, v white fronted-goose Mar/85, garganey May, 18 goosander Mar/85, jack snipe, dunlin. Mute Swans.

Barmere. Private, Cholmondeley Estate, 477535; 26 acres. 30 ft deep; by A49. n ruddy duck, great crested grebe, reed warbler, tufted duck, lesser whitethroat, c 300 feral Canada geese. Winter flocks ruddy duck, c 300 wigeon, 60 shoveler Nov, teal, goldeneye, occasional goosander, Bewick's swan, whitefronted geese, common gull roost, v. cormorants, shelduck, occasional smew, tufted duck, 150 shoveler Nov, goldeneye, pochard, water-rail. Private access via Birchall Town. 10 goosanders Dec/85, a sanderling.

Barthomley. 773524 "Duckeries" marsh-pit.

Betley Mere. A531; 750480. Staffordshire border. n grebes, etc. but disturbed.

Bidston. See Birkenhead. A firecrest singing here May/87.

Birkenhead. Arrowe Park 277864 n rookery, nuthatch, 3 woodpeckers, garden-warbler, tree-creeper, jay, v. kingfisher, hobby 1977, firecrest 1981, siskin, little grebe. *Bidston Hill* 285898, by A553; 230 ft sandstone ridge, mixed woods-gorse. dog-disturbance, n. 43 spp including jay, redpoll, sparrowhawk (and Claughton Ladies' Golf), lesser whitethroat, nuthatch, goldcrest, 3 woodpeckers, tree-creeper, blackap, cuckoo, lesser white throat, bullfinch, grey wagtail 1975, formerly long-eared owl, tree-pipit, woodcock, redstart 1961; siskin summered. v. siskin, woodcock, marsh-tit Dec/85, brambling, wheatear, tree-pipit, occasional pied flycatcher, crossbill, firecrest, nightingale (April), little bunting, Pallas' Oct/80, Bonelli's (May/81 and May-June 1977) and melodious warblers, red-backed shrike, once a buzzard. *Bidston Dock-Pool*: above West Float, Wallasey-Poulton Bridge roads, 299908. n little grebe, coot. v occasional tufted duck, pochard, scaup, Canada geese, cormorant, great crested grebe, divers, kingfisher, Mediterranean, glaucous Dec/85 and laughing (July/84) gulls. Old docks, v black redstart. *Moss & Tip* below M53 & station, 288911, n occasional stonechat, sedge, grasshopper and reed-warblers, reed-bunting, yellow wagtail, meadow-pipit. v snipe, water-rail, swallow-roost, April-ringed Dutch bearded tit Feb/66, nocturnal wader-ringing roost with redshank, dunlin, turnstone, oystercatcher, etc. *Bidston Station Moss:* nest coot, mallard etc, v water-rail, jack snipe, tidal roost 600 redshank, 350 turnstones Dec/85, Iceland gull Apr/85. Bidston Tip is now covered. *Flaybrick cemetry:* v spotted and pied flycatchers, redstart, etc. Tranmere-Rock Ferry prom-Great Eastern-Bromborough Dock, *Mersey shore*: v redshank, curlew, dunlin, whimbrel, jack snipe, etc, swallow and brambling-roost beyond New Ferry baths. Woodside-Liverpool ferry: autumn terns, occasional moulting guillemot, cormorant, kittiwake, little & Mediterranean gulls, but poorer than Seacombe.

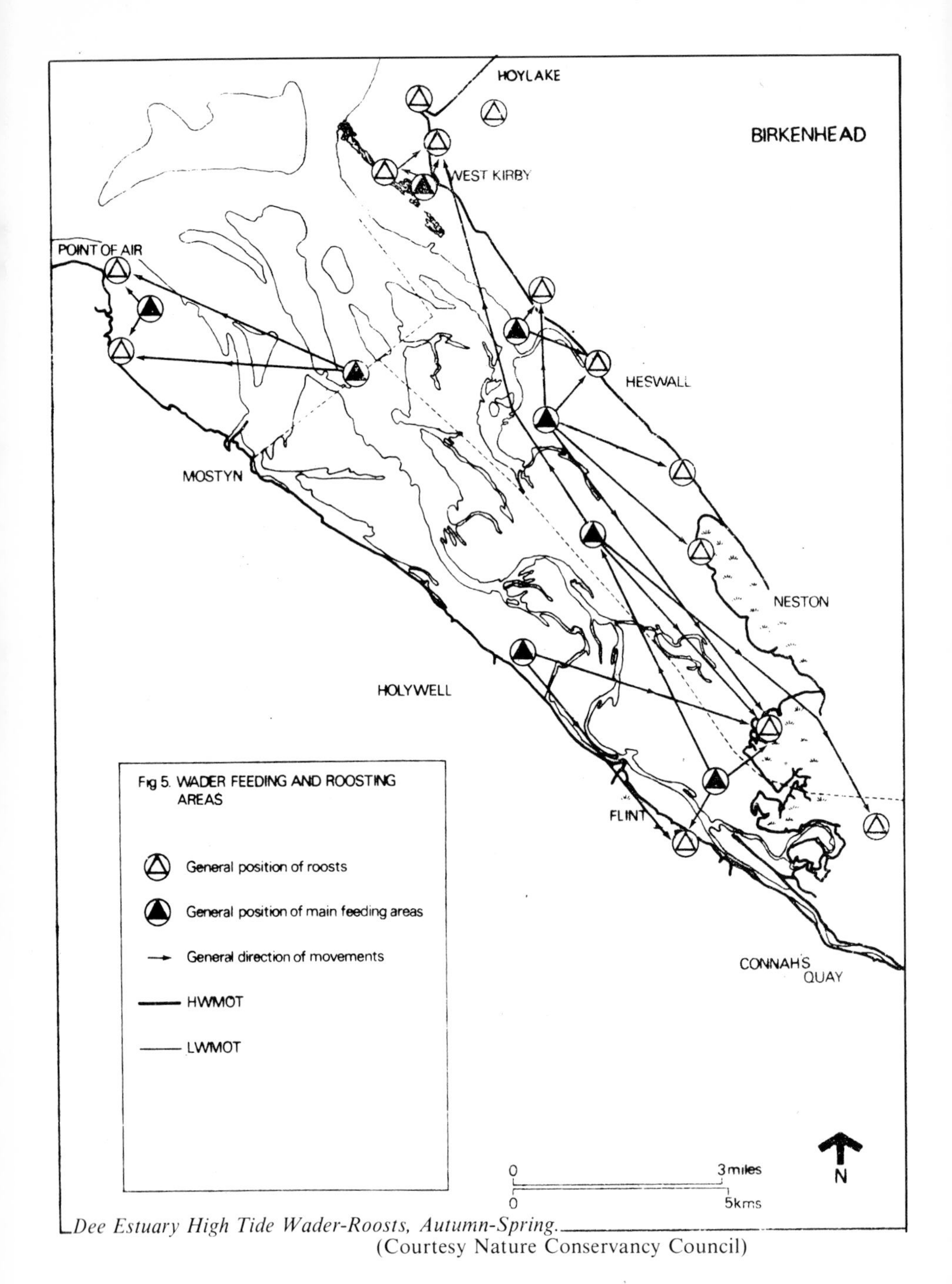

Dee Estuary High Tide Wader-Roosts, Autumn-Spring.
(Courtesy Nature Conservancy Council)

In town, swift & house-martin n. Woodchurch Road; siskin and cole-tit w.v. Temple Road. Tawny owls nest at St. Anselm's Cottage, etc. Spotted flycatchers reared young in 1986 behind a bathroom downspout in Forest Road, Claughton.

Birket Valley. Moreton-Meols, v occasional autumn-winter kingfisher, green sandpiper, herons, etc, floods black-tailed godwits, water-rail, short-eared owl (see Hoylake).

Bollin Valley. n sand-martin, kingfisher, grasshopper-warbler, curlew, dipper, v occasional nightingale. See Cotterill's Clough.

Bosley Reservoir: A523; 921665, over 20 acres. n grebes, sandpiper, redstart. v a few goldeneye, goosander, pintail, pochard, whooper and Bewick's swans, arctic skua gales July/70. Sutton resvr. near Leek Road; Wildboarclough n sandpiper, dipper, green woodpecker.

Bromborough Dock. 349811, spring-autumn HW winds: v little gulls, black, common, little and Sandwich terns. Power-station, n little grebe, stonechat, yellow wagtail, sedge-warbler. To be filled-in.

**Burton.* Dee marshes, via private marsh-road, Burton Station Road-end, 302746, tide 15 mins after Liverpool, 2,700 acres, weedy with sea-purslane, Aster, etc; mostly in Wales. Easiest access Cheshire, Burton or Shotwick Weighbridge private roads. Permits British Steel Corpn. Shotton Works, CH5 2NH 580 acres & Sealand Bank Farm. 38 n marsh & steelworks include: little owl, black-headed gull, twite claimed at steelpools (Clwyd) 1967, sedge, reed & grasshopper-warblers, yellow wagtail, reed and corn-buntings, whinchat, wheatear, stonechat, many meadow-pipits, oystercatcher, snipe, redshank, common, rarely little, ringed plover, mallard, shelduck, occasional teal, shoveler, garganey, great crested grebe, little grebe (rifle-pools), teal 1976, shoveler, little owl, lesser black-backed gull 1938, training wall; 1st Wirral dunlin 1939, 1942. Over 120 v include: 25 Anglo-American waders, 15 early in May. Marsh-End: autumn HW roost up to 15,000 oystercatchers, 5,000 dunlin, redshank, formerly 180 spotted redshank, 38 greenshank, 1st Kentish plover Oct/49, occasional avocet, wood, green etc sandpipers. Formerly one of major British winter haunts of Russian ruff. Over 2,000 moulting mallard, 1,000 winter pintail, 500 teal, 150 wigeon. Duck-pool, rifle-range embankment steelworks corner. Shooting season drives many to Parkgate res. Short-eared owls, winter hen-harriers Oct-May/81 included Orkney-tagged; p.m. marsh and Montagu's summered 1980 with 3 days visit by male, occasional buzzard, hobby, winter merlins, peregrines (roost gasometer), up to 20 kestrels autumn, occasional autumn-winter brent, pinkfooted and whitefronted geese (frost), smew, Bewick's and whooper swans, raven, black, whiskered July/76, occasional Sandwich terns, little crake Jan/73, black-necked grebe, rifle-pools May/72, and Aug-Sept/86 purple heron, spoonbill, red-footed falcon, steelworks, Oct/73, spotted crake, rarely dotterel, glossy ibis, a barred warbler ringed August 1986. A crane spent much of August 1986 at the steelworks, with a black-necked grebe on the rifle-pools. On August 30, 1986 I watched a dotterel on the slag works bank. A red kite flew over the marsh and Puddington 19 Aug/86. A least sandpiper was claimed at the rifle-pools. Winter finches include brambling-roost 30-110, 40 twite, Jan/85, Lapland bunting, occasional water, Richard's and tawny pipits, snow-bunting. Occasional bearded tit, 1973, etc; bluethroat, woodchat and red-backed shrike, white-rumped sandpiper steel-pools July/84. *Burton Pt* (Dog's Nose, marsh-road) v long-eared owl, early March wheatears, etc. Below Puddington Lane, from Burton, where a farm-lane wanders lazily down the map past Burton Barn, a flat, dyke-drained field, the Back Marsh spread out before me from Paddock Wood to the Welsh railway one frosty February day, 1979. My binoculars turned the grey-brown smudge covering half a field into a feeding flock of 1,000 pinkfooted geese. Then, in a pandemonium of voices their long, clamouring skein strung out across the sky. The low-lying, dyke-drained area on the Welsh border called Back Marsh, around Fingerpost Gutter (Clwyd), behind Burton Point (Ness Head), between the railway and Burton Manor Mere (Cheshire), below Puddington Old Hall, the early 18th century Dee river-bed, has been purchased by the R.S.P.B. for development as a reserve. Reached via the farm-lane beyond the school in Burton-Puddington lane, it was the pre-war private duck-shoot of the late Henry Palethorpe where I led many bird-watching field-meeting parties, a marshy, willowy, reedy place with many pools with nesting colonies of reed and grasshopper-warblers, shoveler, teal, garganey, snipe, water-rail, etc, and wintering grey geese, golden plover, woodcock, snipe, etc. Drained early in the war for cultivation, it has recently attracted occasional flocks of pinkfoot geese and is adjacent to Shotwick Lake. A little crake, Dee marshes beyond rifle pools, April 1987.

Burton Pinewood, NT. 314743. NT. Wooded sandstone ridge. n 3 wood-peckers, tree-creeper, nuthatch since before 1930, wood-warbler, long-eared owl June/82, etc. v crossbill, pied flycatcher, firecrest, winter-roost thrushes, finches etc rhododendrons N end. Adjacent Haddon Wood, mixed, 316751, by footpath. n turtle-dove, green woodpecker, sparrowhawk, jay, wood-warbler, shelduck, etc. v woodcock, brambling. Paddock Wd & "Mere", 318738, private angling; formerly n coot, grasshopper-warbler, shelduck, lesser spotted woodpecker, tree-sparrow. Rooks still nest in Paddock Wood, below the manor. Fiddleston Wd, 324747, private, n occasional green woodpecker, redstart, etc. See Denhall; Shotwick Lake.

Caldy Shore. Macdonna Dr. W. Kirby and Croft Rd, below golf-links, 223849. 200-800 winter scaup, Caldy Becks, Dee HW; merganser, 3 longtailed duck Jan/86: 359 black-tailed godwits, Feb/85, turnstone, occasional snow-bunting. Golf-course occasional quail. Woods, n shelduck, great spotted and green woodpeckers, redpoll.

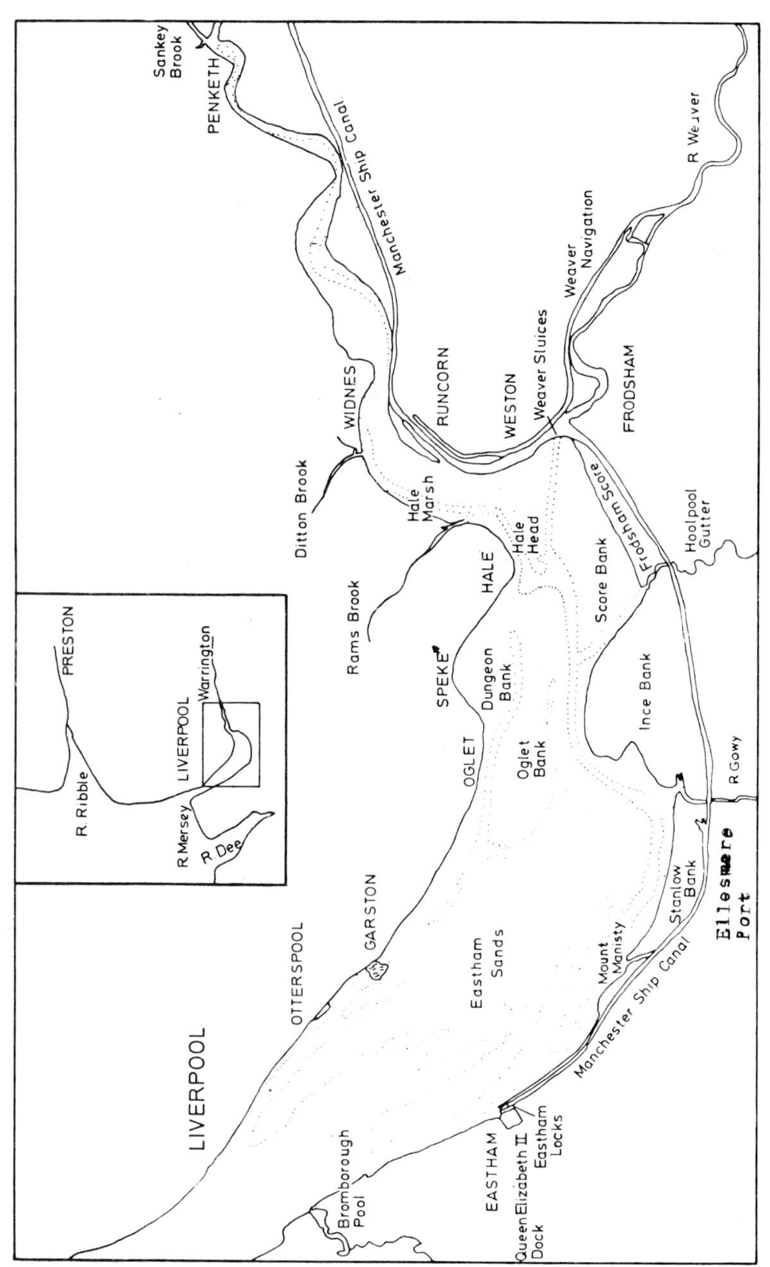

South Mersey Estuary Bird-Marshes, Weaver Estuary & Frodsham Marshes.
(Courtesy Northwest Water Authority)

Capesthorne. See Redesmere.

Cat & Fiddle. 1,690 ft; 001719 via A537 & Goyt Valley. Moorland. n red grouse, curlew, redstart, dipper, ring-ouzel (3 Shires Head), twite, golden plover, wheatear, snipe, tree-pipit, p.m. Goyt, Fernilee (930 ft) resvrs, oystercatcher, wild swans & geese, duck including goldeneye (Trentabank), scoter, etc, crossbill (Goyt Valley), redshank, snow-bunting, merlin, formerly n black grouse, heron. Decline from people-pressure.

Catchpenny SQ. Chelford. 814714. n great crested grebe, v. up to 450 mallard, 50 wigeon Jan, osprey Apr/84. n tufted duck.

Checkley Wood. From A51 near Doddington. Woodpeckers, etc.

Chelford SQ, etc. A535, Lapwing Lane. 814730. n sand-martin, occasional sandpiper, little and common ringed plovers, yellow wagtail, marsh-tit, tree-pipit, woodcock. v mallard, pochard, goldeneye. Farmwood Pool resvr, Joddrell Bank. n coot, Canada geese, tufted duck, sandpiper, great crested grebe. v pochard, goldeneye, shoveler, 195 tufted duck Sept, 40 ruddy duck, Bewick's swan, black tern, black-throated diver Nov/80 and great northern 1982-3, oystercatcher, dunlin, dipper, short-eared owl. Black-headed gull-roost. Astbury SQ. sand-martins. Astle S.F. n dipper, grey wag.

Chester. Dee Meadows, Aldford-Churton-Aldersey, etc, winter floods 425591/416594. v shoveler, teal, 100 wigeon Feb, pintail, tufted duck, Canada & greylag geese, Bewick's, occasionally whooper, swans, water-rail, short-eared owl, occasional white-fronted geese, hen-harrier, cormorants but fewer since banked and part-drained Aldford Brook. Kingfisher and sandpiper n by Dee. *Eaton Park.* Private, 415608, via Pulford, Aldford Bridge and Chester Overleigh Drive. Serpentine Lake: v 20+ cormorants, 9 spp duck include goldeneye, wigeon, pochard, shoveler, gadwall, feral mandarin and snow geese. Oxbow Lake, n heronry 75 nests 1985, 19 after frost 1986, c 50 Duckwood, tufted duck since I recorded them 1938, woodcock, Canada and greylag geese, occasional great crested and little grebe, curlew, turtle-dove, nuthatch, tree-creeper, grasshopper-warbler, 3 woodpeckers, feral mandarin duck and snow goose, barn, long-eared and little owls, snipe, wood-warbler, redstart, goldcrest, long-tailed, marsh and willow-tits. v. siskin, buzzard, cormorant, etc. Eccleston, 412626. n hawfinch, grasshopper-warbler, marsh and willow-tits, little owl, v. firecrest a hobby at Eccleston Aut/85. Handbridge-Overleigh cemetry: hawfinch. Willow tit n and firecrest v Overleigh Drive. Grey wagtails n Chester Zoo polar bear den 1977, spotted flycatcher once cathedral porch, black redstarts City Road works, grasshopper-warbler Chester Kop, mute swan Chester Weir where oystercatchers v; up to 50 (Jan) cormorants roost Dee Roodee racecourse-trees. A hobby visited Eccleston Oct/85. In the big frost, 1986 over 60 cormorants roosted in the trees by Eaton Park Serpentine and a black-necked grebe frozen off the meres was on the Dee below Sealand Road with a wintering Kingfisher. Corn-buntings nest at Handley.

Cholmondeley Park. A49. 554504. Moss Mere 24 acres, part seasonal access, deep marshy Chapel Mere private. n feral greylag and I have counted over 700 Canada geese, etc, great crested grebe, ruddy and tufted duck, 3 woodpeckers. v c400 winter mallard, up to 240 shoveler Nov, 50 tufted duck, 60 goosanders, few teal, pochard, occasional pintail, cormorants, pied flycatcher, osprey May/82, redshank, etc. Here nest ruddy and tufted duck, reed-warbler etc. Herons nested 1985, also green woodpecker, nuthatch, willow and marsh tits. Buzzard and water-rail were visitors. Impressive flights of huge flocks of Canada geese fill the winter sky with their honking cries. Shoveler and pochard winter on Chapel Mere. Whoopers Nov/85, peregrine Jan/85. Mute swans.

Chorlton Water Park. 805934. Mersey Valley, Greater Manchester, v. 40 pochard, 10 goldeneye, escaped ferruginous duck, dunlin, hen-harrier Dec/81, glaucous gull at tip, sparrowhawk. Access via Maitland Avenue, Barlow Moor Road, Chorlton, near Jackson's Boat P.H.

Clatterbridge. B5151. 321824. 1st Cheshire collared dove 1959. Rookery at hospital, nuthatch.

Combermere. Private, 601444. 132/146 acres to 70 ft, deepest west. England's largest private lake, 1½ miles. n ruddy and tufted duck, pochard 1977 (Cocked Hat), sparrow hawk, heronry 40/60 n Great Wood; rookery East Lodge, great crested grebes; snipe, shoveler & black-headed gulls Cocked Hat pool 585435, according to water-level; occasional pied flycatcher & feral shelduck, 3 woodpeckers, marsh & willow-tits, stockdove, goldcrest, garden and reed-warblers, long-tailed tit, nuthatch, tree-creeper, v. up to 700 winter duck of 9 spp, up to 600 mallard, up to 164 ruddy, Nov/83, 5th highest British count, 250 teal and tufted, 50 pochard, 12 shoveler, wigeon, 33 goosander 1982-3, occasional longtail and smew, bittern, buzzard, osprey 1970, I saw marsh-harrier June/77, another Oct/73; water-rail, many cormorants (I found one ringed Puffin Island, North Wales, another from Farnes), occasional divers, black-necked grebe. Ossmere on Shropshire border, 565443, n great crested grebe, etc. v. occasional goosander, goldeneye, diver. Little Marbury Mere n great crested grebe, reed-warbler, tufted and ruddy duck, v. wigeon, shoveler, smew January, black tern. Wrenbury Farmwood Pool v waders, green, wood and common sandpipers, greenshank, redshank, spotted redshank, dunlin, ruff, once great northern diver. One of last lakes to freeze. (See Chelford). Woodcock and Canada geese nest at Combermere where up to 10 goldeneye and 262 coot may be counted in December. Oystercatchers sometimes summer here. A cormorant roost reached 32 in one tree in the

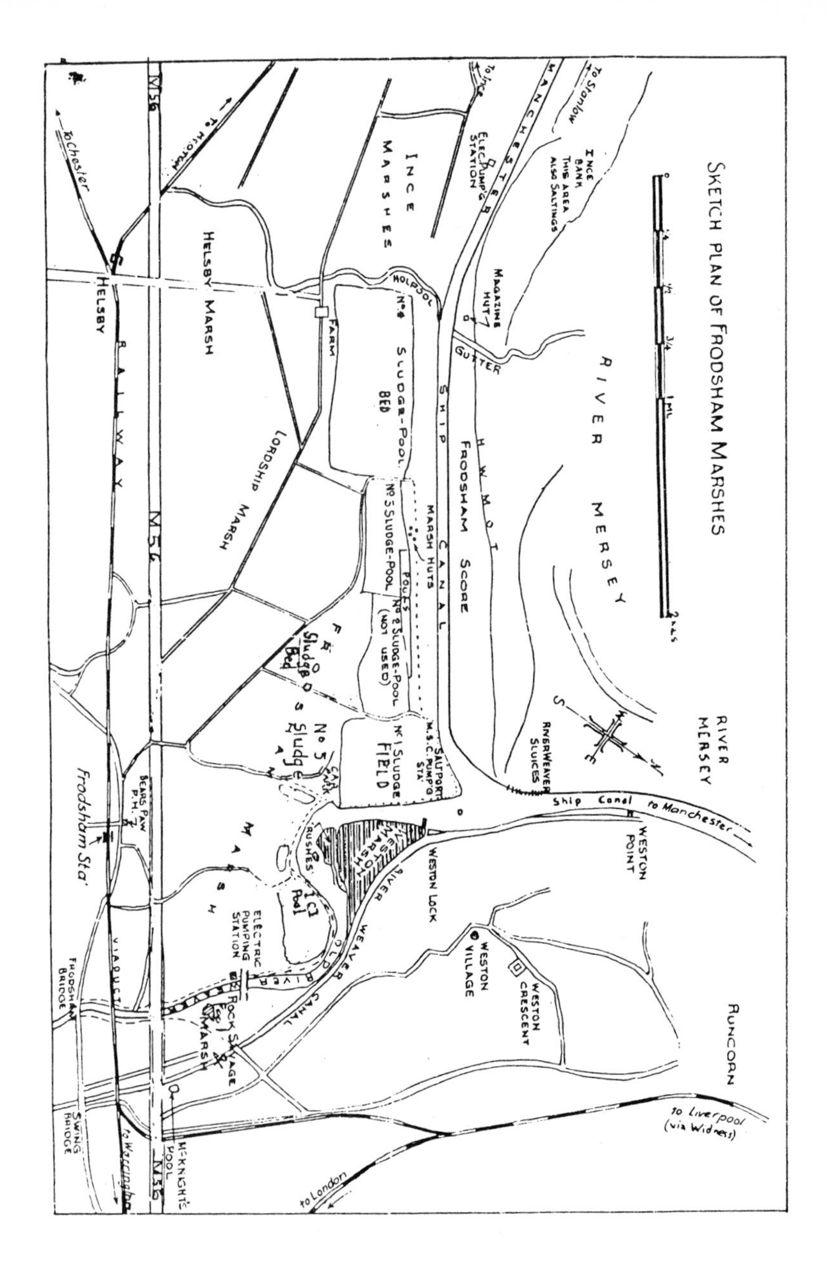

Frodsham Marshes & Weaver Estuary, below M56, via Frodsham Marsh Lane or Ship Street, and Helsby Railway Inn.

February frost, 1986, when 5 smew, black-necked grebe and peregrine were in the park. It used to have nightjars and now has shelduck of feral origin. After 1986 frost I found the heronry reduced to 19 nests. Visitors also include Bewick's swan Jan/85, water-rail, 17 goosanders Feb/85 and 18 goldeneye, shelduck etc.

Compstall. CCT reserve, Etherow Valley 970908. Hide; river, mixed wood, reservoirs, 63 spp have nested including great crested and little grebes, tufted duck, Canada geese, grey wagtail, coot, 3 woodpeckers, occasional tree-creeper, nuthatch, dipper, redstart, garden-warbler, blackcap, marsh-tit, v. teal, pochard, goldeneye, kingfisher, water-rail, pied flycatcher, wood-warbler, green sandpiper, occasional short-eared owl, great grey shrike, alpine swift Aug. 1970, marsh-harrier May/83.

Cotterill's Clough. 802838, Bollin Valley, Castle Mill from A538, CCT, 8 acres. I was an invited guest at the 1935 opening of this reserve, hanging wood & stream where I had previously found it a sheltered "trap" for spring warblers. Nesting blackcap, wood-warbler, goldcrest, grasshopper-warbler, turtle-dove, lesser whitethroat, marsh and willow-tits, with visiting kingfisher, hawfinch, once waxwings.

Crewe Hall. Private. 728548. Former lake and heronry lost in the war. Woods from A434. n nuthatch, lesser whitethroat, rookery. Occasional curlew fields. n redpoll. Oakhanger rookery.

Dane Valley from E Hills with n kingfisher, occasional pied flycatcher; cloughs, Wincle 959661, etc, sandpiper, curlew, little owl, occasional buzzard, sand-martin (Swettenham), redstart, woodpeckers, wood and garden-warblers. v occasional male nightingale. Danebridge 963653, n dipper, tree-pipit, wheatear, ring-ouzel, etc. Danebower: ring-ouzel, golden plover, formerly merlin, etc. High Moor: a few red grouse. Danes Moss, 905703: 28 acres CCT near Gawsworth, pine, birch, oak, bracken, bog, part shot; access footpath old railway N side, some loss to tipping which attracts gulls. n tufted duck, tree-creeper, willow-tit. v teal, snipe, curlew, woodcock, water-rail, short-eared owl, rook-jackdaw roost. Allgrave, A54; 973671, n ring-ouzel, occasional merlin. Gradbach 993658-Goldstitch Moss, occasional merlin, harrier, short-eared owl. Danebower; n dipper, red grouse, wheatear.

Danebridge: Down river bank trees, nesting pied flycatcher, lesser spotted woodpecker, upriver, redstart, etc. Black grouse few Gradbach — Swythamley Hall High Forest; I flushed red grouse Back Moor 1986. Tree-pipit and wood-warbler also nest here.

**Dee Estuary*: 32,000 acres, tidal to Handbridge (Chester) 24 miles. Grade 1 SSSI, 4½ miles-wide mouth, part Wales; shifting channels, sandy shores to Heswall; Spartina, etc. mud-marsh to Burton. A major Sept moulting-ground for dunlin, knot and sanderling. 123

Baird's Sandpiper, a rare American visitor photographed by David Peterson in the Dee Estuary.

regular spp including 22 species of duck, totalling up to 8,000; 3rd British wader-estuary, up to 171,000 H.W. roosts; 3rd major British wintering ground Greenland knot to 48,000 Feb, high tide roosts, declining; 42,500 oystercatchers Jan; 44,671 dunlin Feb; (8th estuary); 809 sanderling Dec and 3,099 spring pm May/72; Denhall to West Kirby 9,000 redshank Sept; the 2nd-3rd estuary after Morecambe Bay; 11,149 bar-tailed godwits Feb (the 10th estuary); leading estuary with 1,300 Icelandic black-tailed Nov, since declined; 4th for 6,700 curlew Aug, 5,500 teal and 15,000 wigeon Dec/85; 6,900 lapwing; 2,627 ringed plover May; 1,293 snipe Dec; 5th with 1,700 grey plover Dec 200 May (5th estuary); 127 spotted redshank Sept/78; 41 ruff July, 30 green-shank; 28 whimbrel Aug; 20 curlew-sandpiper Aug. 8/13th British duck-estuary with 8/12,000 winter, 5.6% of NW Europe; pintail up to 11,265; 3.5% shelduck to 4th nationally 7,315 Oct/80; 10th with 0.4% teal, 0.2% wigeon, and shoveler. It became 3rd for mallard with 5,045 counted Jan/84 and 500 moulting in July; 7th for scaup with 383 Feb/80. Winter roost of at least 47,000 gulls. 80 red-throated divers sheltered Hilbre to Point of Air gales Feb/78. Autumn-passage 1,400 common, 1,000 little (July), 500 Sandwich, Caspian Sept/74, terns. Annual v peregrine, merlin, hen and marsh-harriers, up to 15 short-eared owls, up to 135 cormorants, 41 herons, 300 great crested grebes. See also Hilbre, Hoylake, West Kirby, Caldy, Thurstaston, Heswall, Denhall, Neston, Burton. v Lapland & snow buntings, short-eared owl.

Common tern, a nesting bird on the Dee Marshes. (Photo Eric Hardy)

Dee Marshes. See Parkgate, Denhall, Neston, Burton.

Dee Valley. See Chester. n sand-martins, Farndon, etc.

Dee Steelworks Reserve. Though just in Wales (Shotton — Connah's Quay) this ternery and productive haunt of rarities is most accessible from Cheshire and its records are usually included. In 1957, MNA joined Flintshire County Council, in promoting an unsuccessful by-law to ban Sunday shooting on the Dee which the R.S.P.B. opposed, being then in support of wildfowling with its secretary attending the Dee club. In 1963, after talks with the then owner, and management of the steelworks, I arranged two meetings at Burton Manor of all naturalists and fowlers connected with the Dee. The latter would accept a reserve only on the non-tidal part of the river and this was finally agreed and managed by MRG as a ringing base. It is private -access permits from British Steelworks. See Burton.

Delamere Forest. c 7,000 acres. H.Q. Linmere 551706, via Delamere Station on Chester/Manchester railway, B5152 from Frodsham, and Woodside Lane, Kelsall on A54. Conifers with bog-pools. n 3 woodpeckers, goldcrest, longtailed tit, redstart (including golf-course), occasional pied flycatcher (nest-boxes, Mouldsworth), long-eared owl, siskin 1964 etc, tree-pipit, redpoll, garden, grasshopper and wood-warblers, sand-martin (sand-quarries Mouldsworth, Sandiway, Newchurch Common, Long Ridge, Oakmere), common and little ringed plovers (Shakerley Pools), curlew, turtle-dove, tufted duck, marsh and cole tits, jay, formerly nightjar, nuthatch. v siskins, crossbill, male nightingale, song May/62, Bonelli's warbler June/63, records of melodious warbler, golden oriole etc, male nutcracker 8/68,hen-harrier clearing Jan/85. Hogshead Lane 4-Ways Quarry Pool, spotted redshank, Iceland gull 1984. See Abbot's Moss, Hatchmere, Nunsmere, Shakerley Pools, Oakmere. Tree creepers are common in the forest, several sparrowhawks nest and a pair of goshawks were behind Oakmere Abbey Alms, Hogsback Lane Apr/86 and by Crossley Sanatorium Apr-May.

Denhall Pools. Dee Marshes 294751, via Marsh Lane footpath right bottom of Denhall Lane or Burton Pt Lane. Emerald marshes glistening with pools below Denna Hall-Decca transmitting masts, the resort of winter teal, waders, up to 30 herons etc, few pintail, garganey, up to 20 Bewick's swans frost, whitefronted and pinkfoot geese in frosts, occasional hen-harrier, short-eared owl, tidal wader-roost up to 5,000 oystercatchers, 1,000 grey plover, 400 golden, 127 spotted redshank in autumn-moult, over 20 have wintered; ruff, many snipe, jack snipe, greenshank, a few curlew-sandpipers, little stint, wintering black-tailed godwits, records of buff-breasted and pectoral sandpipers, Wilson's Aug/78 and grey phalaropes, spoonbill Sept/74, occasional brent, Lapland and snow-buntings, twite Oct-March, skuas (gales), mute swan, cormorant, buzzard, hobby, peregrine, sparrowhawk, Greenland wheatear, turnstone, common and black terns, occasional quail (farm). A tidal cormorant roost to 167 Oct/82; dowitcher Nov/70, once a white-winged black tern, occasional Richard's pipit.

Dibbinsdale (Brotherton Park). Wooded valley of River Dibbin, "trap" for spring migrants. Via Mill Lane, Bebington 348827, off A41, or Dibbinsdale Road, Bromborough, 338875. n nuthatch (well-established by 1931), tree-creeper, 3 woodpeckers; I recorded pied flycatchers 1941, 1951, etc.; jay, sparrowhawk, 6 pair of kingfishers along Dibbin including Raby outside dale. w.v. grey wagtail, woodcock, water-rail. Grey wagtail n drainage pipe by motorway 1978. Turtle-dove 1986.

Doddington Mere. Private 718468, 70 acres, by A51 from Nantwich. With Hurleston, biggest inland winter gull-roost. n feral shelduck, Canada geese, great crested and little grebes, ruddy duck, pochard 1981, occasional little ringed plover sandspit, lesser spotted woodpecker, tree-creeper, coot, rookery. Formerly major goosander haunt reduced from 100 to c12 by yatching-angling, likewise 450 mallard, 380 shoveler (Feb), 220 wigeon, 270 pochard, 210 tufted duck, 120 teal, 21 goldeneye Jan, 600 coot Jan, odd pintail, smew, garganey, eider Jan/77, 32 mute Jan and 18 Bewick's swans, whitefronted geese Feb, cormorants included Farne bird, black tern, little gull 1979-81, occasional slavonian and red-necked grebes, spotted redshank, little stint, Kentish Apr/79 and ringed plover, ruff, buzzard (1984), pied flycatcher, Dotterel have been on passage nearby, May. Nuthatches.

Dunham Massey Park. N.T., B5160, Bowdon, 746874 and New Park opposite. Public, 300 acres. n nuthatch, 3 woodpeckers, tree-pipit, tree-creeper, woodcock, occasional redstart, pied flycatcher (outside park 1984), v occasional grebe (pool), Canada geese, tufted duck, merlin. Nearby Brookheys Covert CCT, Sinderland Green, 745904, Hogs Wood, Dark Lane, with v water-rail pond.

Dutton-Aston.573783. Private. Bird's Wood, Long Acre Wood. Dutton Flashes, by Weaver, v waders, including little ringed plover. Mute swan.

A wooded clough in the Goyt Valley, east Cheshire border.
(Photo Eric Hardy)

East Cheshire Moors. Miles of magnificent countryside: hills, streams and cloughs above Macclesfield Forest 974722; Holmes Chapel, Stalybridge, High Disley, Danesbridge 963653, Wildboarclough, Three Shires Head: n haunts of meadow-pipits, curlew, twite (Axe Edge, 025795, Knotbury, Woodhead Moors), golden plover mostly 1,000 + ft; dunlin, wheatear, redstart, short-eared owl (Goldsitch, above Gradbach), fewer red grouse, declining black grouse (Swallow Moss), merlin almost extinct; sandpiper, dipper, grey wagtail; tree-pipit (plantations). Merge into Derbyshire-Staffordshire-Yorkshire

Peak. Arnfield & Swineshaw reservoirs above Stalybridge: twite, golden plover, ring-ouzel, v. merlin, goosander, occasional diver, harrier. Astle Park: dipper, woodcock. Cutthorn Hill: wheatear, ring-ouzel, golden plover. Featherbed Moss, 1,500 ft: golden plover, dunlin, occasional merlin. Low Moor, 0298-0398, best red grouse. Wildboarclough: n dipper, sandpiper, grey wagtail, redstart. Crag Hall grouse-moor (Lord Derby estate) across border: n merlin (1980-

The River Etherow, hunt of dippers, entering Cheshire from the Derbyshire border. (Photo Eric Hardy)

81), long-eared owl, dipper, twite, golden plover, ring-ouzel, occasional harrier. Burchenhough Hill; Flash; Three Shires Head; Woodhead Moss: n twite, red grouse; Crowden (best reached via Greenfield, Chew Valley): n golden plover, dunlin, etc, on Yorkshire border. Royal Cottage; Swithamley; Gunhill-Titterswell over the border, for black grouse. See Cat, Goyt, Bosley Longdendale, Macclesfield; Knotbury 018682, Holy Moor (merlin); Blaze 974676. A golden eagle was over the Woodhead Tunnel and Pulford-Chester, Apr/85 not from falconers' birds — kept at Wrenbury (flown near Cholmondeley) and Stalybridge. Hobbies summered and merlins nested near Axe Edge, 1985. Buzzards nest occasionally near Danesbridge and peregrines near Alport Castle above Snake Roach. Blackcock lek at the Long Hill, Swallow Moss, with ring-ouzel and wheatear nesting nearby. Black grouse are now believed extinct in Cheshire. Wheatear and curlew favour Shutlingslow. Red grouse and ring-ouzel are over the border at Axe Edge. Teg's Nose, Langley has nesting pied flycatcher. Goldsitch red grouse, ring-ouzel; Shining & Castors red grouse, oakenclough, wheatear, winchat; Cheeks Hill, Whetstone Ridge, Ridgegate.

The River Goyt leaving its reservoir on the Derbyshire-Cheshire border, a haunt of dipper and grey wagtail. (Photo Eric Hardy)

Eastham Wood. 364818 public; information office; deciduous, much birch; large beeches attract bramblings during winter incursions, n 3 woodpeckers, nuthatch (nest-boxes), sparrowhawk, jay, marsh-tit, wood-warbler (May), occasional pied flycatcher, hawfinch, firecrest Nov/83, marsh-warbler June/79 hawfinch/79. *Job's Ferry*, 365818: Mersey tide 25 mins later than Liverpool, up to 50 winter cormorants, occasional shag, up to 64 great crested grebes. I counted 13,548 black-headed and common gulls in 1½ hrs February afternoon passage to upriver roost; v. occasional Mediterranean and little gulls, laughing gull Nov/77, ring-billed gull 1984; black-necked grebe Feb/76, autumn terns, occasionally black. House-martins n. Ship Canal lock-buildings; dead little bittern April/84. *Rivacre-Wood* n. turtle-dove, green woodpecker. v records roller, great grey shrike.

Eastwood: 12 acres RSPB, Stalybridge, 972977, urban; hides, ponds, warden. n blackcap, jay, tawny owl, spotted flycatcher, cole-tit, tree-sparrow, green woodpecker, grey wagtail. v little grebe, woodcock, dipper (winter), pochard, goldcrest, sparrowhawk, nuthatch, water-rail.

Eaton Park See Chester.

Ellesmere Port. Little ringed plover nested in Shell oilworks 1979, Roller and great grey shrike have visited Rivacre Woods.

Etherow Country Park. ST 965909, off A626 near Manchester, east of Stockport. Woodland with canal and river-marsh.

Farmwood Pool. Jodrill Bank, Lower Withington, A535, 814730. n great crested grebe, tufted duck, etc. v grebes, 200 coot Dec, 195 tufted, 105 ruddy duck, shoveler, pochard, goldeneye, black tern, occasional short-eared owl, Bewick's swan, black and red-throated Jan/85 and great northern diver Dec/82, black-headed gull-roost. Black-necked grebe is a winter visitor. Canadas.

Fiddler's Ferry, Power Station. Old Lancashire side of Mersey. See my "Bird-Watching in Lancashire" (Dalesman 1979). Map Ref. 550855-535857. Lagoon with winter flocks shoveler, wigeon, mallard, pochard, tufted duck, pintail, scaup. Gulls include Iceland and glaucous. River marsh with teal, curlew, short-eared owl, scaup scoter, rarer waders. Nesters include sand-martin, common and little ringed plover, redshank, stonechat. By canal reed and sedge warblers, sandpiper, kingfisher, once by power station black redstart. Visiting peregrine roost on tower where kestrels nest. Little grebe greenshank, scaup, etc are also visitors. Private. Towpath access Marsh Lane to Richmond Bank and Gatewarth tip. Oyster-catcher, shoveler, coot, shelduck, corn-bunting, partridge, yellow wagtail, etc. nest in area. Visitors include marsh-harrier, ruff and other waders, garganey, gadwall, longtail duck, 600 mallard, 250 pintail, 186 shoveler, 300 curlew, 1000 teal, 400 wigeon, 60 stockdoves, black tern, hoodie crow, Bewick's swan, water-rail, n tufted duck, SF.

**Frodsham-Helsby Marshes* 518779; 13,500 acres dyked, reclaimed fields. Access Frodsham Marsh Lane & bridge over M56; Helsby 798494 Railway Inn, Lower Rake Lane. Pumping Station pools by Ship Canal, SSSI. n grasshopper, reed and sedge-warblers, little grebe, whinchat. v goldeneye, water-rail, early garganey, occasional spotted crake, bearded tit, grey phalarope, bittern, marsh-harrier, red kite Aug/64, probably the bird lost by a West Kirby falconer, also May/75, Apr/76; swallow-roost, occasional whitefronted and pinkfooted geese, overwintering common curlew — once buff-breasted, and green sandpipers; little stint. Old sludge-deposits decline as dry-out. Tufted duck and black-headed gull n 1952. v frequent pectoral (autumn, occasionally spring) occasional buff-breasted, wood, sharp-tailed Aug/83, Baird's Apr/71, marsh, broad-billed May/75, and white-rumped sandpipers No 5. No 1: 1-5,000 golden plover including northern race. Up to 9 short-eared owls. I first drew attention to this area 1930 and with late Dr. F.J. Manning made a 1939 survey of Ince Marsh before wartime oil-terminal expansion. There were pre-1965 records of smew, turtle-dove, goldeneye, sparrowhawk, great skua, goosander (Feb/42). It borders Weaver estuary (q.v.) Over 200 spp; n meadow-pipit (21 pr 1967), yellow wagtail (16 pr), occasional ringed and little ringed (ICI sludge) plovers, corn-bunting, redshank, little owl, variable whinchat, stonechat, snipe, sand-martin, lesser whitethroat, low bush magpies, turtle-doves. v finch-flocks; a brambling-roost during incursions, Savi's warbler May/81 and May/79, yellow-browed warbler Oct/86, twite, water-pipit (Dec), occasional snow and Lapland-buntings, bearded tit Oct/81, red-backed shrike, records of icterine Aug/78, 1971, Savi's May/78 & aquatic Aug/75 warblers, Richard's pipit, black tern, harriers, bittern, little bittern Aug/70, lesser white-fronted goose Jan/83, rough-legged buzzard Oct/75, lesser golden plover claimed Oct/72. c 500 dunlin and curlew-roost sludge-beds spring tides; one of north's 3 major roosting grounds of up to 150 Russian ruff autumn; grey plover, godwits, 1,000 ringed plover Aug, 3 phalaropes, whimbrel, spotted redshank, dotterel (Aut/83, previous May), Kentish plover Aug/82, spoonbill (occasionally March), Temminck's stint, turnstone, long-billed dowitcher Sept/70, stilt-sandpiper Apr-Oct/84, stone-curlew Oct 171, sharp-tailed sandpiper Aug-Sept/83, up to 5,000 lapwings Jany. I noticed a lesser yellowlegs 7 Sept/1953, published it in Liverpool Daily Post on the morning of 14 Sept; then the record published in a local Birkenhead school society bird-report claiming "discovering" it there on 14th Sept! Ortolan bunting May/73. Pratincole April 28, 1987.

In Feb 1942 late J. Lord (Merseyside Nats Association, later editor Midland Bird Report) recorded goosander, red-breasted merganser and two smews on No. 3 sludge-bed, with pochard, shoveler, tufted duck and black-necked grebe. In Aug 1953 imm. little gulls (3), curlew-sandpipers, little stints, 1 grey plover, ruffs, etc. (E.H. Liv. D. Post.) Osprey and broad billed sandpiper visited No. 4, May/87.

Feral flamingos, quail, records of spotted crake, little bittern (Aug), purple heron Mar/29, crane Apr/54, 15 little gulls March, whiskered tern June/70, white-winged black tern Nov, merganser 1942, smew Feb/42, goosander 1942, goldeneye 1942, etc, pochard, pintail, mallard, tufted duck, black-necked grebe Aug-Oct/42 (from Abbot's Moss), merlin, peregrine, sparrowhawks, fewer hen-harriers than Dee, Montagu's (May also June/83) and marsh; buzzard Oct/81, hobby, a long-eared owl-roost 1984. The Twiggery, 495772, is a private reed-tree-dyke reserve. Kingfishers nested at the Ship Canal Red Bank 1984. Osprey visitor April 1987.

**Frodsham Score*. Restricted access, high bank by tidal Mersey marsh, Ship Canal 490788, NE of Holpool Gutter's muddy estuary. Occasional n oystercatcher, redshank, major haunt shelduck; v occasional brent, Iceland gull, waders, teal, pintail, wigeon flocks, but less than downriver Ince Bank; rough-legged buzzard Nov/78. 72 Shoveler, frost Jan/85. See Weaver Sluices. An avocet was here Sept/84.

Frodsham-Helsby NT Hills. Wooded sandstone-ridges, above Castle Park (rookery, nuthatch, etc) 514766 and A56 Helsby 491752. n nuthatch, 3 woodpeckers, tree-creeper, turtle dove, corn-bunting, lesser whitethroat, jay, redpoll, wood-warbler, cole-tit, swift in cliff, Helsby 1942. v hoopoe Helsby July/77; hawfinch, pied flycatcher (May).

Gayton Sands. See Heswall, Parkgate.

Goyt Upper Valley 015725. Derbyshire border reservoirs, moorland cloughs, Goyts Moss. Access Pym Corner (car-park) A5002 from Whaley Bridge to Goyt's Lane car-park and A537 Derbyshire Bridge-Goyt's Clough car-park. Shining Tor 1,833 ft. Cat's Tor (995738), 1,703 ft. People and boating pressures; weekend car-restrictions beyond car-parks, but minibus. n ring-ouzel, golden plover, woodcock, teal, dipper, sandpiper, whinchat, redstart May-Aug, twite to 1,500 ft., tree-pipit, grey wagtail, green woodpecker, long-eared owl, once pied flycatcher, formerly merlin, declining black grouse. Upper Goyt, heron Fernilees resvr 1958, etc. v woodcock, crossbill, hawfinch, brambling, merlin, osprey, merganser (nested Errwood 1977). Hobbies nest on the Derbyshire side since Coward's old account. See East Cheshire.

Greasby Brook. 247868. Field-roost tidal waders below Pump and Wood Lanes autumn-spring: golden plover, green sandpiper, 200 redshank, 50 curlew, etc.

Great Budworth Mere. See Marbury Park. 3 or 4 pairs of herons returned to their pines Apr/86 where 3 nests used 1985.

Hale. On former Lancashire side of Mersey, not to be confused with Hale in Greater Manchester. See my "Birdwatching in Lancashire" (Dalesman 1979). Mainly tidal duck and waders. Map Ref. 477813-478826. With others, I watched a citrine wagtail on the Mersey marsh, Within Way end Apr/86. n. occasional redshank, ringed plover. Duck decoy used for ringing with up to 500 winter mallard, teal etc, little grebes, occasionally nest, kingfisher etc, shore marsh, Halegate Road, golden plover, greenshank, swans, godwits, grey phalarope etc. Greenland white-fronts, Oct/81, pintail. n. teal. Garganey visited Ramsbrook pool May/87.

Hatchmere. 555723, B5152. n great crested grebe, tufted duck, coot, reed and grasshopper-warblers, v pochard, goldeneye, occasional bittern, etc. Boating.

Helsby. See Frodsham.

Heswall. Dee shore via Gayton Cottage Lane (800265). High tide autumn-winter, hen-harrier, short-eared owl, c30-80 water-rails, finches include twite, brambling, linnets, etc. Riverbank, Seabank and Delavor Roads or footpath from Parkgate north prom-end car-park. Gayton Sands RSPB £225,000 reserve stretches from Moorside Avenue, Neston along Parkgate shore to Heswall Gayton. v water-pipits, up to 70 rock-pipits, 25 twite, Dec-March, over 1,000 curlew October tides, shore-larks wintered 1982-3, and one was near Parkgate Mar/77, little bunting field ponds Jan-Apr/83, Lapland and snow-buntings, glaucous gull (yacht club), curlew-sandpiper, 400 stockdoves Nov-Dec/83, wader-roost, up to 900 black-tailed godwits winter. Gales bring great skuas. Summer feeding common terns, occasional little; teal winter in shore-gutter. Grasshopper-warbler n occasionally Heswall Hills and Dales; ring-ouzel, woodcock, and quail occasional v Dungeon. Winter shore-fields with short-eared owl, merlin, hen-harrier, sparrowhawk. Nightjars still n in friend's garden at The Dales, 1949, before urbanisation. Hawfinch, red kite Aug/82 and raven have been recent visitors.

Hilbre. Cheshire's best seabird-watch. 3 tidal sandstone outcrops in Dee mouth; main island 200 ft. 11 acres, seawards; tide 16-20 mins earlier than Liverpool. Access permit and leaflet, Leisure Dept, Wirral BC, Station Road, Thurstaston L61 0HN. Best seawatches

Oystercatchers, from a hide on Hilbre Little Eye, as tide recedes.
(Photo Eric Hardy)

HW, onshore W-NW winds July-May; summer trippers numerous. All islands low tide access on foot; start 3 hours before HW according to height of your wellies or thigh-boots, from bottom Dee Lane, West Kirby, 1 mile. Head between Middle and Little (upriver) island or left of Little Eye, not direct to main seaward island; then follow track either side Middle Hilbre to main island path, left corner. Beware slippery wet rocks. Return via far(river)side Middle-Little Eyes 2 hrs after ebb. Shorter low-tide visits leave main island not less than 3 hours before HW. Erect photographic hides (best weekdays with fewer disturbing visitors, or early morning tide) 2 hrs before HW, Little Eye N end tide-line (oystercatchers, sanderling, knot, godwit, dunlin), Middle Island N end rocks (turnstones), Main Island NE bay near Lion Rock (turnstones); guys can be nailed into soft sandstone. Public watching hide N end main island, key from custodian (white cottage). Up to 16 little gulls have been seen in autumn, 120-150 in Dec/75. Green woodpecker, Tanskey Rocks Apr/87.

232 spp; n meadow pipit, skylark, occasional blackbird, song thrush, formerly wren now aut-winter v., wheatear & shelduck (Middle Eye, where feral pigeons n 1934-5). In 1945 herring-gull nest and eggs brought by youths from N. Wales. Formerly kestrel and robin nested. v regular divers, grebes, including slavonian Jan/53, Nov/54, Jan/55 & 57, Oct/63, Apr/76; black-necked Nov/46, Dec/58, Sept/81, fulmars, 5 shearwaters including little Sept/84, Cory's May/76, Great Oct/71. Leach's petrels autumn gales (I recorded c 1,000 in Liverpool Bay Sept/52 & 957 Dee Mouth Aug/78), gannet, grey phalarope, turnstone, purple sandpiper (laminaria-zone below old lifeboat-house and E. shore), over 3,000 bar-tailed godwits Little Eye Jan/85, kittiwake, little, Mediterranean, ring-billed Aug/82, Bonaparte's, laughing and other gulls, 4 skuas, terns including black, and Royal accepted Sept/74, a Caspian claimed May and June 1986; hobby July. Auks (chiefly guillemot and razorbill) and passerine-movements including goldcrest, chaffinches, up to 62 whinchats in July, 13 twite. Movements with Calf of Man, Formby Pt, and Walney Island. In Nov/51 MNA picked up a male blackbird main island, ringed 14 days earlier on passage near Jaeren, S. Norway. First shore-lark 1905, then 1953. Best Cheshire site for purple sandpipers, shag, occasional eiders; a glaucous gull came for 15 years, feeding low tide rocks, high tide inland at West Kirby tip. We had 8 Sabine's gulls 1963-84, 11 snow-buntings Oct/47, 4 Bewick's swans Feb/39, 20 in Mar/59, 22 whoopers Nov/56, barnacle-goose Apr/40, gadwall Feb/56, velvet-scoter 1971 & 72, surf-scoter Nov/69, 80 mergansers Dec, 8 pomerine skuas 21/10/84, little stint Oct/34, Oct/50, curlew-sandpiper Oct/34, spotted redshank Dec/53. A wood-sandpiper flew calling over me, LT Aug/68, an osprey Oct/76. In hard winters I've seen song thrush and redwing breaking winkles against rocks. 44 migrant spp 19/5/62 included 111 Manx shearwaters, 61 kittiwakes, 51 fulmars, 35 gannets, 22 scoter, razorbills, guillemots, Leach's

Knot, redshank, dunlin and oystercatchers from a hide on Hilbre Little Eye, December 1969. (Photo Dennis Green)

petrels, 3 Greenland wheatears, goldcrests, etc, flying E in strong wind. Gull-billed tern Oct/82, white-winged black tern Oct/82, serin Apr/76. An early swallow, probably male by its long tail-streamers was confirmed 13 March 1986, a fortnight after an exceptionally early one in Anglesey. Over 60 species seen in one day autumn, woodcock and magpie Oct/86.

In Oct/34 I organised the first visiting bird-watching party for now defunct Liverpool field-club; in 1935 I wrote an article on its birds in The Times, in 1939 an account in Hoylake & West Kirby official guidebook and organised first experimental wader-ringing with clapnets prewar. In 1935's Associated Learned Societies' exhibition in Liverpool Technical College, I exhibited model Heligoland trap and plans for Hilbre bird-observatory and ringing station (*Nature* 2/Nov/35). In Dec/45, MNA published an open letter to the Council on the future of Hilbre and in 1950 held a meeting in the island coastguard-room to promote an observatory, using the old lifeboat-house; but Hoylake UDC declined to agree, having plans for public visitors. In 1957 a ringing station was established independently. In 1982, Liverpool University published a comprehensive book on Hilbre (see also review, Liverpool Daily Post 13 May/82). See West Kirby, Hoylake. 130 Manx shearwaters Aug/86.

Knot and dunlin at Hilbre Little Eye, high tide. (Photo R. Warhurst)

Hoylake. Red Rocks (Hilbre Pt), Stanley Road-end, 203884, tide 17 mins earlier than Liverpool. Dryshod views HW waders, especially autumn. Sea-watch, gales: shearwaters (Sooty, Cory's), auks (occasional little, puffin), arctic, great, occasional pomerine and long tailed skuas, velvet-scoter, terns include roseate, Forster's (Sept/84), autumn black terns, glaucous and 50 (March) little and Mediterranean gulls, red-necked grebe Mar/76, gull-billed tern, Red Rocks Aug/71, May/76, Beach Road July/82: wry neck Sept/83. An early red-spotted blue throat landed at Red Rocks in full view from the sea 25 March 1986, then flew off towards Hilbre. An early record of 15 whimbrel were there March 6. Spring passage white wagtails; records of shore-larks, snow-bunting, red-throated pipit, red-rumped swallow May/84, black-billed cuckoo claimed Oct/82, *Bird Rock*: offshore for HW photography, if no sea-anglers or covered by 10m tides in strong NW wind. *Shore* to W. Kirby: HW wader-roost up to 30,000 knot and dunlin Jan, 5,000 bar-tailed godwits and oystercatchers Oct, 1,300 black-tailed godwits, May-June peak sanderling (fewer when disturbed by dogs, horse-riders); ringed, occasionally Kentish, plovers, snow and Lapland buntings. I've seen light and dark-breasted brent at HW. *Beach Rd* (off Stanley Rd); HW waders, curlew-sandpiper sanderling, ring-billed gull July/82, laughing gull July/83. *Shore Marsh,* CCT: n sedge, reed, grasshopper-warblers, reed-bunting, occasional stonechat. v water-rail, occasional spotted and little (Jan/73) crakes, short-eared owl, jack snipe, a recorded great reed-warbler May/75, bearded tit Oct/72, cirl bunting Nov/76, aquatic warbler Aug/76, garganey, etc. Golf-course corner poplars; rarer migrant passerines, early mornings autumn, included red-breasted flycatcher, bluethroat, common and black redstarts, woodlark, red-backed shrike May/79, yellow-browed, melodious, barred and aquatic warblers, also wryneck, hoopoes, etc. On dunes, occasional short-eared owl, hen-harrier. Inland bee-eater appeared June/83. Red-rumped swallow and dowitcher were by Red Rocks corner Oct/85 and a gull-billed tern below Beach Road July/82, merlin Red Rocks Aug/75, and 7 short-eared owls, marsh-golf course Nov/78. Records of red-throated pipit and aquatic warbler, occasional pied flycatcher.

(*Huntington Reservoir*. 428628. n great crested grebe, mute swan. v black tern, duck include a few shoveler, occasional goosander, scoter, waders including ruff, occasional slavonian grebe, autumn starling, swallow and pied wagtail roosts. n sedge-warbler.)

Hurleston Reservoir: Bache House, A51, Nantwich, 620555. n great crested grebe, reed, sedge and grasshopper-warblers. v small flocks tufted duck and pochard, black tern, waders (green sandpiper, green shank, ringed plover, jack snipe, woodcock), occasional osprey, water-rail, bearded tit Nov/61. Little grebe, tufted duck and lesser spotted woodpecker nest here. Many gulls roost here in winter when water-rail and willow-tit are visitors also little gull Aug and Bewick's swan Dec/84. Sludge-beds visited by dunlin, glaucous gull Jan/83; 3 goosanders Jan/85. Twite, Dee/86.

Huxley Pools. 508604. n great crested grebe, ruddy duck.

**Ince Bank*. 775460, Mersey marsh off Ince Gorse, Ship Canal; restricted access. n oystercatcher 1984, redshank, etc, over sq mile sea meadow-grass exposed HW except spring tides, major night-feeding wigeon (2,650 Dec) and dunlin-roost (28,000 Jan), also 1,000 curlew Mar, major flocks lapwing, redshank, golden and grey plovers, 4,350 shelduck Feb, 9,000 teal Nov, a few shoveler, occasional little stint, 100 common ringed plover, sanderling, little ringed plover, knot, ruff, jack snipe, turnstone, godwits, whitefronted and pinkfooted geese, Bewicks's swan, garganey, 44 stockdoves Feb/84, shore-lark Mar/83, peregrine, merlin, buzzard, short-eared owl, avocet Aug/84, rough-legged buzzard, in gales Leach's petrel, fulmar, great and arctic skuas, autumn terns including black, glaucous gull Dec/74, water-pipit, rock-pipit, occasional goosander, hoodie crow Feb/85. See Mersey; Stanlow.

Ince Gorse: Sandstone gorse-covered outcrop, restricted causeway access from Stanlow Point or Frodsham Score. v twite, snow-bunting, siskin, etc. n oystercatcher, shelduck, redshank, lapwing.

Ince Marsh: Industrial fields inland of Ship Canal.

Kingsley Sludge-Pool: 560765, Weaver Bank, footpath from Hall i'th'Hay Farm below Ball Lane; silting; former n site little ringed plover overgrown. n great crested and little grebes, tufted and ruddy duck, grasshopper-warbler, corn-bunting. v 200 teal, shoveler, pochard, goldeneye, snipe, green and wood-sandpipers, ruff, grey and red-necked phalaropes, lesser yellowlegs Sept/71, Savi's warbler June/78, kingfisher, Bewick's swan Feb/82, kittiwake gale Oct/83. Warburton Wood, CCT; Crewood Big Wood (private). A bird-reserve is planned at the pool.

Knutsford Moor. 756792; 36 acres, c 40 spp, reedbed S end of Tatton Mere; n reed, sedge and grasshopper-warblers, green woodpecker, turtle-dove, mute swan. v swallow-sandmartin roost Aug-Sept, pied wagtails Sept, starlings Dec, corn-buntings. v water-rail, bearded tit Apr/81. *Heath* 748788; 36 acres, bushy old sandpit, n. yellowhammer, linnet, willow-warbler. v 3 woodpeckers, goldcrest, long-tailed tit, 40 spp. *Boothsmere* 785768, Longridge Rd, n Canada geese v pochard etc. *Mere Mere* 733826, 42 acres, 100 ft deep, private, 40 winter pochard. Mobberley Lake 785794, B5085, n Canada goose, yellow wagtail, curlew in area, occasional woodcock, v 11 spp wader including occasional black-tailed godwit, redshank, ringed plover, green and wood-sandpipers, dunlin, snipe, little stint, greenshank, sanderling, little ringed plover. See Tatton, Tabley. Knutsford Mere with reeds, below the car-park, has tufted duck and grebes, etc. with the Dog Wood path into Tatton Park. An SSSI.

Langley Reservoirs, Macclesfield. 946715; 600 ft. n tree-pipit, red grouse, redstart, heron, dipper. v 15 goldeneye (Dec), goosander, cormorant, black tern, Bewick's swan, marsh-harrier. Trentabank: slavonian grebe May/80. Ridgeway Resvr 953716. Herons n occasionally Key Wood, Romiley, and Trentabank reservoir, pied flycatchers in boxes at Tegg's Nose. A pair of goshawks failed in a 1986 nesting attempt. n Canada geese.

Leasowe Bay (922268). Occasionally n ringed plover 1983/4 top bank; tidal roost 250 turnstones, redshank, sanderling, dunlin, oystercatcher stone breakwater islets. Gull-roost HW Squibbs Factory field by railway. Occasional hen-harrier, black guillemot Feb/84, great crested grebe, grey phalarope, little, Mediterranean and Sabine's gulls, auks (storms), purple sandpiper, spring Bewick's swans, snow-bunting, shore-lark, black redstart, winter stonechat. Woodcok visit Ditton Lane, and lesser white throats nest. Leasowe Common-hedged market-gardens: short-eared owl roost, woodcock visit Ditton Lane, and lesser white throats nest. 33 Leach's petrels, a storm petrel and a great skua flew off the promenade in 2½ hours, hightide gale Oct/86, early wheatears; n grasshopper-warbler. See Meols. 2,850 knot 1,250 dunlin and other waders roost on the breakwater islets at high tide. Sooty shearwater Sept/86.

Little Budworth Mere. 559656. n grebes, ruddy duck, grasshopper-warbler, v teal, etc. See Oulton. A country park, map ref. 590655 with birch-heath and nesting tree-pipit, redpoll, etc, off A49.

Little & Big South Marbury Meres. 560455. n Canada geese, willow-tit, little grebe. 26 ruddy duck and visiting pochard, goosander, marsh-tit. Twite Dec/86.

Liverpool Bay/Rock Channel. The Cheshire sea, via yachts, fishing boats, Liverpool-North Wales Sept cruise, etc; 16½ miles Seacombe-Bar Light. c300 moulting guillemots autumn; flocks kittiwake, little, glaucous, Mediterranean, etc, gulls spring & autumn. Seabird-passage: gannets Feb-May, July-Oct Manx, up to 50 Balearic, sooty, great and Cory's shear-waters, 2-5,000 autumn "comic" terns, also black; 4 skuas. Passerine movements: barred warbler Sept/66, tree-sparrow, pied wagtail, "willow-chiffs", chaffinch, robin, wren, wheatear, goldcrest, also barn-owl, common sandpiper, etc. One of Britain's highest autumn tern concentrations.

Longdendale Valley reservoirs: River Etherow, Tintwistle, Low Moor (grouse). 025973. Longdendale Moor and scree, 750 ft. Woodhead Moss (twite), Crowden, edge of Peak National Park moors. n curlew, golden plover (Shaw Moor), twite (feed pastures below moor), whinchat, redpoll, dunlin, tufted duck, little owl, stonechat, black-headed gull, willow-tit, Canada goose, green woodpecker (pine-plantation). Declining red grouse (Hollingworth Hall moor, 980995), formerly merlin, nightjar (Broadbottom). v migratory flight-line: mallard, occasional goosander, wigeon, scoter, scaup, shoveler, goldeneye, short-eared owl, hen-harrier (Dec), occasional hobby (Sept), buzzard, osprey, bittern, kingfisher, cormorant, whooper and Bewick's swans (Feb), red-throated diver, heron, woodcock, green sandpiper, little ringed plover, siskin, winter flocks 200 twite 1,000 ft Molinia (grass) moors, with snow and Lapland buntings. See East Cheshire, Tintwistle. Dunlin nest on moors.

Lyme Park: NT, 1,320 acres to 964 ft Derbyshire border moors. Best entry Higher Poynton 945834 or Disley 966844 n redstart, woodcock, curlew, green woodpecker, wood-warbler, v occasional black grouse. People pressure weekends. 8 a.m.-dusk; car-park.

Lymm Dam. Local reserve. A56; 681869. n great crested and little grebes, etc. v tufted duck, pochard, occasional cormorant, bittern, black-necked grebe Oct/78, marsh-harrier Dec/46, goosander Mar/72. Bradley & Mag Brooks, The Bongs (Woods), Dingle. n tree-creeper, nuthatch, long-tailed tit, great spotted woodpecker. v kingfisher. Car-park and ranger-hut behind church.

Macclesfield Forest. A537. 974722. Moors. n twite, dunlin, redstart, wheatear, ring-ouzel, tree-pipit, woodcock, long-eared owl (High Moor firwood), declining black and red grouse. Wildboarclough: n dipper, grey wagtail. Shutlingslow Farm to Summit, Piggford Moor (private). Ridgegate resvr v goldeneye, occasional slavonian grebe and longtailed duck. Sutton resvr, Leek Road, black-throated diver Feb/85, goosander. See Bosley, Cat, East Langley, Goyt. Dunlin nest on moors; raven and goshawks visitors.

**Manisty Bay, Mount Manisty*. 394789. Artificial 150 ft mound of Ship Canal excavation, Mersey shore part of MNA Stanlow reserve. Access restricted. n 1st Cheshire oystercatcher 1936, collared dove, meadow-pipit, corn-bunting, occasional little owl, pre-war wheatear. v green and lesser spotted (Oct/74) woodpeckers, great grey shrike, siskin, willow-tit, snow-bunting, twite, water and rock-pipits, shorelark, jay, 40 common terns May and autumn tides, gadwall, Iceland gull, great skuas Nov/77, kittiwake July/76, Jan/76, Jan/78, shelduck, summer-moulting flock drake mallard. Spartina beds v short-eared owl, up to 28 herons, woodcock, water-rail. Poole Hall gutter, N end, occasional tufted duck. 150 black-tailed godwits wintered 1984-5. See Stanlow. From the summit of Mount Manistry in January frost one looks down upon an enormous view of captivating colour — miles of glittering Mersey marshes edged with ice where the wild brightness of the sun spreads beneath the raw blue of the spacious sky beyond Stanlow Point with the white stack of Hale lighthouse and over Ince Bank to the harsh outline of *Helsby* Hill. At sunset nearly 200,000 gulls gleam into view like a mile of snow, packed to roost in midriver. On May 23, 1936 I counted 612 birds of 43 species including 57 shelduck and 5 ringed plover stonechat, yellow hammer, whitethroat and partridge all of which bred locally.

Marbury Country Park, Great Budworth mere with 14 acre reed-bed. (CCT). 651768, via Cock Inn Lane-end footpath 655774, or Comberbach Lane 651762 car-park. n great crested grebe (30-100 birds March), tufted, ruddy, occasional shoveler ducks, reed and grasshopper-warblers, reed-bunting, heron (1984), in pines, turtle-dove. Wooded side: nuthatch, tree-creeper, marsh-tit, redpoll. v 99 shoveler Feb, 88 teal, pochard, wigeon, occasional goosander, scaup, eider Jan/64, 13 goldeneye, divers, cormorant, red-necked grebe (frost), black, common, Sandwich (Aug) and once whiskered terns, occasional bittern, night heron May/82, little and glaucous gulls, water-rail, kingfisher, 380 coot (frost), firecrest, house-martin 23/11/58. Butterfinch Bridge ICI lane-pools. 651762. n little ringed plover, grasshopper, etc, warblers, lesser whitethroat. v dunlin, green and wood sandpipers, greenshank, water-rail, ringed plover, curlew-roost, occasional short-eared owl, little stint, avocet, great grey shrike, up to 23 little ringed plovers July, many snipe. See Northwich, and Little Marbury. v great northern and black-throated divers.

Meols-Leasowe Promenade. 234907-256916. Major sea-watch onshore aut-winter gales. v arctic, great and pomerine skuas, Manx, (12 on 9/9/76) Balearic, occasional sooty, great Sept 80 and Cory's (Sept 80 and Aug/81) and little Sept/85 shearwaters. I was 'phoned a graphic description of an albatross (possibly, not proven, black-browed), 2 ft bigger than nearby gannet, immediately after my friend, Dr Stuart Thomas, saw it in storm Sept/78. Riding the wind in flapless flight, this huge white seabird, dark above, light below, with heavy, hooked beak and fulmar-like eyes, wedget-shaped tail and wide wings, dwarfed nearby gannets. 230 + great crested grebes in frost 1971. Up to 50 Leach's petrels (Maderian claimed 1984), little auk, kittiwake (including May), Mediterranean and Sabine's gulls, (Franklin's claimed), up to 65 little gulls spring; auks (including black guillemot records), slavonian (Jan/85 & Feb/77), 2 black-necked (Oct/71) and red-necked (Jan/84) grebes; bar-tailed godwits, spring Bewick's swans, kingfisher Sept/75, occasional scaup, longtail, eider, velvet-scoter. Kestrels have n in old lighthouse and nearby Cadbury's factory. *Leasowe Common – Meols Market-Gardens;* fields inland of prom: grey phalarope Sept, occasional May dotterel, ring-ouzel Mar-Apr, white wagtails spring, great grey shrike, desert-warbler Oct/79, twite, grey crow, black redstart, red-breasted flycatcher, arctic and yellow-browed (Oct/84) warblers, snow-bunting, up to 10 short-eared owls (declining) roost now declined since ploughing, lesser golden plover claimed Sept/76; pectoral sandpiper Sept/70. Carr Lane, inland side railway: n yellow wagtail (blue-headed n 1954), grasshopper-warbler (and Park Road), occasional corn-bunting. Reed-beds behind Carr Lane brickworks: grasshopper & reed-warblers, reed bunting, v. little grebe, snipe, jack snipe, bee-eater June/83; see Moreton, water-rail, green sandpiper. River Birket: v green sandpiper and spotted crake, autumn, kingfisher, winter. Railway Station Pond: occasional HW diver, grebes, scaup; less often since angling. See Leasowe, Moreton.

**Mersey Estuary*. 40 sq. miles (12 less than Dee), 22 nautical miles like a greasy serpent from Wallasey-Warrington; sheltered, ¼ mile wide Narrows, Birkenhead, where 5-6 knot tide floods into a widening, curving muddy bay 3 miles wide at Stanlow, taking 1 hr 50 mins to flow, more to ebb, exposing 37 sq miles at low tide, 33% densely inhabitated with tiny Macoma shellfish food. 2 sq miles eroded in last 10 years. Sheltered from W winds by North Wirral factories and from disturbing access by Manchester Ship Canal. My "stamping ground" since schooldays where my wildfowl research began in 1932 when a fowler gave me a Russian ring from a mallard shot wintering at Stanlow. In 1947, as regional organiser of the new National Wildfowl Counts, I arranged monthly counts at all local haunts, which revealed the greatest concentrations on the Mersey. In 1970, as MNA's contribution to Conservation Year, I negotiated Cheshire's biggest bird-reserve on Stanlow Marshes, between the Gowy estuary and Poole Hall Gutter. Subsequently, a threefold increase in teal, wigeon and shelduck with mallard and pintail nearly doubling, raised it to international importance. The south (Cheshire) side of the inner estuary has consistently varied with The Wash and Inner Solway as Britain's major duck-estuary, with up to 22,000 to 70,000 duck (Feb) and 21 spp, as well as with 140,000 gulls roosting with 14 spp, and 10th British wader-estuary with up to 53,268 of 58 spp. Some 2,000 migrating "commic" terns feed on autumn sprat-shoals,

The shore of Mount Manisty a Mersey haunt of waders where Cheshire's oystercatchers were first found nesting. (Photo Eric Hardy)

despite a chemical cocktail laced with lead, mercury and sewage as black as a glass of Guinness. White-winged black tern, New Ferry-Seacombe rarely. Wigeon graze the sea-washed turf, *Puccinellia maritima* at night where it spreads in acres on Ince Bank and off Frodsham Score, and roost on Stanlow Bank. Pintail feed off Stanlow, Ince, Manisty and Weaver Sluices. Curlew roost Ince-Stanlow, lapwings Ince Bank and Stanlow. Dunlin peak in December, curlew on autumn migration. 40,000 waders were here in winter 1980-1. Redshank, lapwing and oystercatcher nest on Ince Bank. Shelduck here feed on polychaete worm Pygospio, Macoma, Nereis and Hydrobia; mallard on Macoma and Hydrobia; pintail on small crustaceans, seeds of Salicornia and Spergularia, etc. The record count of grey plover reached 537 off Ince-Stanlow after the big frost March 1986. Up to 92 little gulls have been counted at the river mouth Oct/76 and 632 Apr/87 with over 100 white wagtails.

Peak flocks bring the sky alive with wildfowl late Nov-Feb. The leading British estuary for pintail with 18,450 Nov/80, it has 45% of British and 17.6% European counts; and for teal, up to 35,000 (Dec), it has 35% of the British counts and 7.3% of NW Europe. It is 2nd for shelduck with up to 11,800 (Dec/81), 4th-5th for wigeon with 15,300 (Dec), 4th for dunlin with 46,000 Feb/81 and 12th for mallard with 8,000. A few shoveler, gadwall, occasional merganser, goosander, goldeneye and tufted (in frost). Grebes, cormorants, peregrine, merlin and short-eared owl also winter, with visiting grey geese (now usually pinkfeet) and wild swans. Storm-sheltering seabirds enter the mouth. There's some interchange with Dee pintail, shelduck and dunlin according to gales, probably with Ribble pintail too, and duck flight to Prescot, Knowsley and inland Cheshire. As on the Dee, Scandinavian *alpina* dunlin winter, Greenland *arctica* and Icelandic *schinzii* mainly late spring, etc, passage-migrants. A few godwits, grey plover, knot, twite, rock-pipits, ruff, many lapwing and nationally-important qualifying counts of 1,070 redshank, 1,200 curlew, and golden plover occur. Tranmere oil-jetty had tufted as well as shelduck in frost Jan/85. See Eastham, Frodsham, Manisty, Moss Side, New Brighton, New Ferry, Runcorn, Seacombe, Stanlow, Wallasey, Weaver, Woodside.

Middlewich. Two Gate Tarn.

Mollington Mere. Home Farm Lake, 388704, private, shallow, n little grebe, Canada geese, sedge and grasshopper-warblers, mute swan (and at Backford) v heron, etc.

Moore. See Moss Side, Heronry formerly Green Wood now scattered and reduced to c4 1986. A vast new tip here will attract gulls.

Moreton Brickworks Flash, via Lingham Way railway-footbridge 254906, or foothpath-end of Tarran Way South, around fence beyond gas depot, below Station 259908. 30 ft deep claypit, gull-washing haunt, replacing similar prewar MNA little grebe reserve, since filled-in, nearby brickworks. n coot, great crested and little grebes, mallard, tufted duck, reed-bunting, mostly failing from vandalism; occasional sedge and reed-warblers, lesser whitethroat; house-martins from houses other side of railway feed here. v 15 spp duck, chiefly 18 tufted, occasionally to 122 pochard, teal, ruddy, garganey, goldeneye, gadwall, wigeon, scaup, scoter, smew Apr/86, escaped ferruginous and red-crested pochard, green sandpiper, little ringed plover, jack snipe, black tern, slavonian grebe Jan/85, Bewick's swan Oct/84, short-eared owl, water-rail, spotted crake; Franklin's claimed Nov/81, ring-billed July/84, Mediterranean July-Oct/84 and glaucous gulls, Bewick's swans Oct/84, etc. ortolan bunting Oct/83, black-throated diver and brent goose Feb/86, kingfisher, turtle-dove, merlin, willow-tit, little bunting nearby Cadbury's factory Oct/83; a quatic 10/87 and grasshopper-warblers; willow-tit, firecrest (farm-lane hedge); red-throated pipit, field Tarran Way Oct/84, bearded tit Nov/77, water-pipit, stone-curlew, fields June/59. Redpolls n nearby Kestrel Rd gardens. See adjacent Leasowe, Meols. A slavonian grebe was here Feb/85 and an exhausted American nighthawk found near Pasture Road in October. This 6½ acres water may be filled in 10 years. Angling is increasing. Carr Lane brickworks pools off Birkenhead Road, Moreton-Meols has nesting reed and sledge-warblers in reed-beds, and visiting redshank ruff, green sandpiper occasional bittern and a penduline tit 14 Sept/86. See Meols. Meadow-pipits n fields.

Moreton Hall Park. A34 4 miles S.W. Congleton. N.T.

Moss-Side. Lapwing Lane end, A558 Moore; 569855; n whinchat, stonechat, sedge, reed and grasshopper-warblers; blackcap, shelduck, occasional teal, shoveler, redshank, long-eared owl, 3 woodpeckers, turtle-dove; 1st Cheshire garganey n 1957 adjacent (since-drained) Halton Moss 570848. little ringed plover. v stonechat, siskin (alder-wood) Old Quay canal 578858; bearded tit n. June/81, Apr/84, to 2,000 lapwings, 1,000 teal, 21 curlew, water-rail, to 7 short-eared owls, 9 long-eared owls Jan-Feb/85, marsh-harrier, merlin, pectoral sandpiper (Halton Moss), 19 Bewick's swans spring, 200 wigeon, garganey, occasional pinkfoot geese, Franklin's gull Jan/84, Cheshire's first little bunting Mar/56, black redstart Apr/84, grey crow, water-pipit, snow-bunting, great grey shrike, arctic skua, gale Nov/87, herons from c30 n Keckwickford Green Wood 561840. Interchange with Fiddler's Ferry-Richmond Bank, opposite side of Mersey. 5,000 fieldfares, many redwings (30% Icelandic), frost, on windfalls, Daresbury Fruit-Farm. A proposal for massive tipping at Moss Side has an alternative 200 acres reed and wet land proposed as a future reserve, West of Lapwing Lane.

Neston. 2 miles out into Dee marshes, Fisherman's Path low tide from Moorside Lane-end 286769. Reed-bed (n reed-bunting, sedge and occasional reed and grasshopper-warblers). v water-rail, once bearded tit (Apr/82), jack snipe, etc; autumn swallow-roost, bittern, 38 shoveler Oct/84, Field-path behind Library, Beechways Drive, to Old Quay and sewage-works outfall 286766. v to 70 water-pipits autumn-winter, rock-pipit, twite. Or gutter-path out ebb from "Harp", Marshland Road-end, Ness, 290762. v shelduck moult-migration evening flights July-Aug; HW up to 135 cormorant-roost, 25,000 oystercatchers and other waders moving up river or roosting marsh tide-line. Hen, occasionally marsh, harriers, peregrine, merlin, occasional buzzard, white wagtails March, black tern, spotted crake. See Parkgate, Burton, Dee.

New Brighton. 313934. Low tide shorebirds and HW gale sea-watch, Mersey mouth, v 200 Leach's petrels aut/78, Manx, Cory's Aug/80, sooty and little (Oct/77) shearwaters, little auk (Oct/38), occasional gannet, fulmar, grey phalarope; kittiwake, little, 4 Sabine's Sept/78, Mediterranean, 30-years-old wintering Iceland, bottom Magazine Lane, where ring-billed June/82 and ivory claimed June/26, gulls; cormorant, occasionally shag, autumn; great northern diver Oct/82, guillemot, razorbill (Egremont Oct/81), tern including black, autumn, white-winged Aug/72; 4 skuas, great crested grebes winter, occasional eider. Lighthouse Rocks-Egremont, LW up to 300 turnstones, a few purple sandpipers. Wader-roost HT, new sea breakwaters. Marine Lake: occasional goldeneye, longtailed duck, scoter, cormorant, merganser, little gull, great crested grebe; 9 waders, up to 20 purple sandpipers, when drained. Cobbly shore below promenade, Perch Rock-Egremont "Beehive": redshank, curlew, turnstone, dunlin, knot, oystercatcher, bar-tailed godwit, ringed plover. Disturbed by bait-diggers and dogs. Snow-bunting Nov/84. HW breakwater-roost off King's Parade and lighthouse. House-martins n promenade. We watched a rough-egged buzzard by railway-side cutting Oct/55 until it died of aspergillosis in lungs. See Seacombe. Up to 70 kittiwakes have been counted and 16 little gulls in February; October curlew-sandpiper and storm-petrel, skuas, in high tide westerly gales. 80 bar-tailed godwits March/87.

New Ferry. "Great Eastern" shore-bank, 343856. LW waders, dunlin, ringed plover, curlew, whimbrel, little stint. North side, Rock Ferry Parade. August swallow-roost & winter brambling-roost, willows below New Ferry baths. Old slurry-bed (declined as overgrown) HW roost up to 500 redshank Sept, 200 ringed plover and 3000 common terns Aug, 70 curlew, 40 bar-tailed godwits Oct, 30 turnstones, 6 whimbrel, 1,000 dunlin Jan, occasional ruff, curlew-sandpiper, sanderling, shelduck, gadwall, longtailed duck, pectoral sandpiper May/73, cormorant, occasional shag, spotted redshank, bearded tit July/60, short-eared owl, winter grey wagtail, shore-lark, snow-bunting. HW outside and inside private (Levers) Bromborough Dock 349850, becoming disused. Up to 200 autumn common, occasional Sandwich, little and up to 14 black terns; white-winged black tern Aug/73; kittiwake, little and Mediterranean gulls; laughing gull claimed Aug/77. Reed-warblers have nested by pool.

Norley SQ. 578728. n sand-martin. v. occasional Bewick's and whooper swans. Corn-bunting nests Sparstow, etc.

Norbury (Cholmondeley) Meres. 560494. 250 teal Feb. 70 shoveler Nov. 45 wigeon Jan. Goosander.

Northwich Flashes. 655755/665755, waste lime and salt subsidence; Witton, Neuman's, Woodbridge, Marston, etc. Despite the hostile industrial area with n little ringed plover (Witton, etc, 664745), attempted ringed plover, reed and grasshopper-warblers, v stilt sandpiper 1984, Caspian tern claimed July/67 and July/81, 500-1,000 curlew roost autumn, golden plover flocks, once Wilson's phalarope, great snipe claimed May/76, Handley floods; spotted redshank, regular green and wood sandpipers, water-rail, black tern, Iceland gull, autumn little stint, occasional short-eared owl. Roadside Pool, 673671 near Marston Church: few tufted duck, teal, pochard, waders. Also Lostock. Tip-gulls include great black-backed. Billinge Green pools: n tufted duck, grebes, redshank. v waders including ruff, pochard, winter curlew flock, Baird's sandpiper May/55. Saltersley Moss n sand martin, v little ringed plover, short-eared owl Nov. Shakerley Leisure Centre (old sandpits), Sandiway, Sandimere. n sand-martin, coot, Canada geese, willow-tit, redpoll (birchwood). v scoter, waders including greenshank, dunlin. Allostock 745708, n yellow wagtail, little ringed plover, sand-martin, corn-bunting, v 250 curlew Feb, snipe, wader, redwing-roost. Former Plumley Ascol Lane Pools, CCT reserve, 765752 with former n little ringed plover, now overgrown. n reed and grasshopper-warblers, willow-tit, woodcock, lesser whitethroat, turtle-dove, red-legged partridge, formerly redshank. See Marbury. Franklin's and Iceland gulls, broadbilled sandpiper and a claimed needle-tailed swift May/87.

Nunsmere. 586685. By A49, private, 30 acres deep, old sand-quarry, wooded edge of Delamere Forest which, in 1968, I professionally helped previous owner design for a conservation award. n black-necked (1984) great crested and little grebes, tufted duck, formerly little ringed plover 1969-73, green woodpecker, turtle-dove, v ruddy and tufted duck, etc. Sensitive to water-levels, black-necked grebes previously nested at nearby Abbots Moss, Oakmere and Rostherne. See Delamere. n tree-pipit, bull finch, Canada goose.

Oakmere. 575675, Private, shallow, peaty, wooded lake by A64 and back lane fields behind Harrington caravans. Owner: Sandy Brow, Tarporley. No outflow. Heronry (no nests 1984, 18 in 1985, 12 in 1986). I found pochard n 1972 (2nd Cheshire record) and in 1941 black-necked grebes on separate small, reedy arm. Also n redstart, tree-pipit, willow tit, great crested grebe, v 100 teal Feb, goldeneye, longtail Oct/66, green sandpiper, black kite June/80. Oakmere Sandpit, 574680. Nearby 4-Ways Quarry by Hog's back Lane behind

The 'arm' at Oakmere, a former nesting haunt of black-necked grebes.
(Photo Eric Hardy)

the Abbey Arms has nesting sand-martins and little ringed plover Goshawks were nearby in Apr/86.

Ossmere. 564443, Shropshire border, n grebes, v duck occasional diver, etc.

Oulton Park.Mere 696647 private, n great crested grebe, tufted duck, reed warbler, nuthatch, stockdove. v to 200 tufted duck, 100 pochard, 9 goldeneye occasional smew. See Little Budworth.

**Parkgate.* Tidal Dee marsh, includes 5,000 acres, £225,000 RSPB Gayton Sands reserve from Moorside Ave-Heswall (Warden, Burton Cottage, Denhall Marsh Lane). Public car-park 273788 via Boathouse Lane, with winter roost to 7 hen-harriers opposite (one Orkney-tagged), up to 80 water-rails flushed from Spartina beds by HW, occasionally perching golf-course bushes; spotted crake; wader-roost 4,000 redshank, 2,000 curlew July, 1,000+ grey plover, 14,000 knot Dec, Icelandic black-tailed godwits, bar-tailed; 50 greenshank Aug-Sept. Tidal flights pintail, 3,500 shelduck, wigeon, mallard, etc, c1,000 teal in offshore gutter (which precludes transect of marsh nearer than Moorside Ave, Ness). Kingfisher, common, occasionally arctic, Sandwich terns; stockdoves, 3-4 merlins Aug-April, peregrine, occasionally hobby, great grey shrike, Iceland gull.

spotted crake, jack snipe, spotted redshank. Winter finch-flocks up to 2,000 brambling with chaffinch, linnet, 50 twite, greenfinch, tree-sparrow, once serin, feed shore spartina, roost high hedge golf-course-shore-edge footpath to Gayton Cottage Lane; 30 water pipits, rock-pipit; white stork Oct/83. Wirral Way, sheltered shrubby old railway-cutting from car-park path. See Dee, Heswall, Neston,Wirral Way.

Peckforton Hill. Wooded sandstone ridge, part public Sandstone Trail from Beeston 538582, Bulkeley 531554, Upper Burwardsley 530570; Tattenhall Station-Belswood Park. n. pied and spotted flycatchers castle side & Bulkeley Hill, wood-warbler, woodcock, nuthatch, redstart, 3 woodpeckers, barn and little owls, sparrow hawk, goldcrest, cole tit, turtle-dove, tree-pipit, grasshopper-warbler, marsh-tit, formerly buzzard. Nuthatches are common and garden-warblers nest annually. Nightjar calling nearby Burwardsley June 1986. Firecrest, Nov/86. Tattenhall Ponds attract winter wigeon. Bickerton Hill, n tree-pipit, etc.

Petty Pool. 620698. Wooded mere. n tree-pipit, willow-tit, great crested grebe, woodcock. V occasional goosander, black tern Aug, some disturbance.

Poynton Lake. 923845. By A523. n great crested grebe. v tufted duck, gadwall, shoveler, pochard, (claypits), dipper stream, tree-pipits.

Prestbury SF. Declined wader-haunt. v green sandpiper, dunlin, twite, water-pipit, once Lapland bunting; pied wagtail roost.

Quoisley Meres. 546456. CCT. n great crested grebe, tufted and ruddy duck, reed-warbler, v teal, shoveler, tufted, garganey, occasionally bittern, water-rail, goosander. See Marbury South.

Rabymere. 332813. Disturbed. n little grebe 1984. v kingfisher, (n Hargreaves Hall Farm 1980-4), tufted duck, heron.

Radnor Mere. 846762. A 34, Nether Alderley. n great crested grebe, tufted and ruddy duck, woodcock, 2 or 3 nests of heron. c 400 winter coot 40 ruddy duck, 303 teal, Dec, 60 pochard, shoveler, goosander, wigeon, black-headed gull-roost. See Alderley Edge. L.S. woodpecker.

Reddish Vale. 905925. v jack snipe, little grebe, great grey shrike Dec/83, waxwings 1982, occasional waders, duck.

Redesmere. 848714. n great crested grebe, tufted and ruddy duck, reed and garden-warblers, lesser whitethroat, redstart 1973, 3 woodpeckers, water-rail, red-legged partridge. v black-necked grebe summered 1980, 300 coot Dec, 120 tufted Oct, ocassional longtail, honey-buzzard July/73, water-rail. Boating. Capesthorne Hall Fishponds: 845725. n great crested grebe, ruddy duck, woodcock, mute swan, v duck. (angling). A little gull was here Oct/85. A whiskered tern Sept/74. n goldcrest, Capesthorne.

Risley Moss, Birchwood, Warrington. Formerly Lancashire and covered in my "Bird-Watching in Lancashire". n. woodcock, long-ealed owl, formerly nightjar. v hobby (autumn), hen-harrier, etc. Old peatland with bracken, birch, pines. Map Ref. 665918. Rixton Claypits have winter duck.

Rock Channel. See Liverpool Bay.

Rocksavage Pool. See Weaver.

Rode Heath, Rode Pool. 815575. Junction A34/A5011. Private. n great crested grebe. v pochard, tufted and ruddy duck. Rode Hall, 808574, private small heronry. Lawton Hall Wood & Lake, 825556, private. n nuthatch, ruddy duck, mute swan.

**Rostherne Mere*. NCC. Biggest and deepest mere, 118 acres, 105 ft deepest; shallowest SE; reed-bed and woods; off A556, Restricted; public access churchyard 743837 with viewing seats; hide £2, warden Rowans Cottage above church. c 200 spp, 66 n, including 6 pr great crested grebes, (up to 56 birds July), mallard, teal, shoveler, ruddy duck, 32 pr reed-warblers but seldom sedge; marsh and willow-tits, little owl, woodcock, occasional tufted duck, water-rail, corn-bunting, yellow and grey wagtails (Rostherne Brook), black-necked grebe Gailey Bog 1939. Biggest county inland winter haunt mallard, up to 4,000 Dec, etc, especially frost when last of meres to freeze. v 1,000 teal, 910 tufted frost/82, over 2000 mallard, 2100 pochard

Rostherne Mere a Cheshire bird-reserve. (Photo W. Blore)

Feb/86 with 6 velvet-scoter in frost movement from East to West, 3000 pochard and 180 ruddy duck in March. 1072 tufted duck. In 1986 a record 50 pairs of reed-warbler nested. 398 wigeon, 400 pintail Dec, 290 shoveler, 76 ruddy duck Dec, 22 goldeneye March with 4 smew Dec-Jan, goosander, gadwall, etc. Some recent decline in pintail, pochard, etc. c 250 Canadas with some from Salop, Staffs and Yorks, and feral greylags, occasionally wild pinkfoot and white-fronted geese, up to 98 Bewick's swans spring; up to 3 buzzards Sept, occasional hobby, marsh and hen-harriers, osprey March/81, red kite March/79, black tern May and Sept, white-winged and whiskered claimed; occasional bittern, black-necked grebes from Nunsmere, occasional red-necked; siskins, hawfinch, bearded tit Nov/77, occasional great and arctic skuas, grey plover, turnstone, sanderling, purple heron July/77, Maderian little shearwater July/77, occasional spring and summer kittiwakes in winds. Sept-April roost of 80-100 cormorants from Cheshire and S.Lancashire waters, 20,000 gull-roost of 7 spp winter, including occasional glaucous, Iceland, little and Mediterranean. Laughing gull claimed Dec/84. Autumn starlings roost reeds; winter woodpigeons, stockdoves. See NCC handbook on mere. 10 little gulls were here May/85; 24 goosanders Jan/74. n. green woodpecker.

Royden Park. See Thurstaston.

Runcorn Gap. 104,000 gulls counted passing through to roost lower Mersey estuary, afternoon Jan/83. Manx shearwater in storm; starlings roost bridge. Most panoramic view Mersey Frodsham marshes from A557, Weston, and Rose Cottages below Weston Village Cross, 508801. Dock tip, 495813: n common and little ringed plovers. No Man's Land now eroded. Runcorn Sands: v teal, shoveler, up to 4,300 pintail Dec, 650 shelduck, 230 mallard, occasionally longtail, little ringed plover, jack snipe. Ring-billed gull Old Quay Dec/84. Carrion-crown sometimes on bridge. Floodbrook Wood, CCT, 800533. See Astmoor, Moss Side, Weaver. Little grebe, coot and nuthatch nest in Runcorn Town Park Blackcap and garden warbler visit Pickering's Rough near Norton and Windmill Hill. Information, warden, Norton Priory. Feral greylag geese nested by Ship Canal 1980. A great skua appeared in a gale Oct/86 over the Mersey flying upriver. Shoveler n Wigg Island, 1987; a visiting marsh -harrier May.

Sale Water-Park. 811926. n tufted duck, occasional shoveler, little grebe. v sandpiper, common and arctic terns, stonechat, rock-pipit, grasshopper-warbler, goldeneye, smew, great crested, red and black-necked (Feb/85) grebes, little ringed plover, Bewick's swan, water-pipit, cirl bunting (Jackson's Boat Oct/84), black-throated thrush Nov/83, Montagu's harrier May and Sept/71. Boating disturbance. An occasional escaped ferruginous duck appears between Mersey and M63 near Jackson's Boat P.H. See Chorlton.

Saltersley Peat-Moss. CCT. Wilmslow.

**Sandbach Flashes*. CCT, 150 acres, 7 salt-subsidence waters. Watch Lane below Elworth Station, 728608. Elton Hall, Clay Lane 720590, best for pintail, little ringed plover, etc, little bunting Sept/67, upland plover Dec/83. Railway Flash, Clay Lane, 717586, restricted footpath, pintail, pochard, wigeon, spotted sandpiper Sept/80, Sept/82, little egret June/82 and May/84. Pump-house, Elton, restricted, occasional smew, goldeneye, stilt-sandpiper May-Oct/84. Fôdens, Plank Lane. v long-eared owl. Warmington, Green Lane, 706613. Crabmill, 708606. Winterley, A534. 150 spp., n reed and grass-hopper-warblers, little ringed plover, redshank, tufted, ruddy and feral shelduck, shoveler, great crested and little grebes, lesser whitethroat, Canada goose, mute swan, stockdove, little owl, heron 1977. v black-headed gull-roost, little (March) and Mediterranean gulls, black and white-winged black (Aug/69, June/82) terns, to 900 teal Dec, 500 pochard Jan, 170 wigeon, 60 coot, 50 pintail, garganey, gadwall, longtail, shoveler, occasional Bewick's swan, white-fronted geese, 80 dunlin, many ruff, golden, Kentish, ringed and grey plover, pectoral, white-rumped, stilt (1984), wood and curlew-sandpipers, occasional summer green sandpiper, godwits, stints, whimbrel, oystercatcher, many aut-winter snipe, occasional sanderling, dowitcher Oct/72, semi-palmated sandpiper Oct/71, Oct/75, lesser yellowlegs Watch Lane Aug/74, avocet Apr/74, Wilson's (Sept/70) and red-necked phalaropes, spotted redshank, turnstone, water-rail, spotted crake, merlin Sept-Oct, occasional hobby, great grey shrike, marsh-harrier May/84, spoonbill, lesser white-fronted goose Jan/76, hobby at starling-roost June/73, occasional spotted crake, avocet, dowitcher Oct/70, lesser yellowlegs Aug-Sept/74, cirl-bunting Apr/75.short-eared owl, cormorant, occasional winter bittern, red-necked grebe, water-pipit Oct/78, swallow-roost. A decline in recent years. Arclide Quarry pool: eider Feb/83. Several waterfowl "escapes" not listed. Water-rails nest at Foden's and Elton flashes. Good access via Station Road, Fodens and Red Lane, ahead at Clay Lane for Elton Flash. We saw 2,800 Lapwings at Watch Lane (Red Lane) Flash Aug/86. Up to 100 magpies have roosted in winter. A red-throated pipit in May 1976. n grey wagtail.

Sandiway 694687. Whitegate Way, Newchurch Common. n sand-martin, near golf-course.

Sandstone Trail. 538582, Beeston. See Peckforton.

Seacombe. 325908. HW autumn-winter estuary-watch, sewer at promenade above ferry and by tunnel-ventilator. Sheltering from NW gales 30 Oct/79 were 20/30 arctic, 6 pomerine and 5 great skuas, 3 Sabine's gulls, 3 Manx shearwaters, 3 fulmars, 3 red-throated divers, gannet, etc. v to 30 black terns (Aug), white-winged Sept/74, occasional roseate, once whiskered; Leach's and storm-petrels, Mediterranean, Bonaparte's Aug/79, glaucous and up to 20 little gulls, occasional red-necked and great crested grebes, longtail duck and passing scoter, merganser, goldeneye, cormorant, heron, merlin. Stonechat, whinchat, black redstart, Lapland and reed-buntings visited nearby Scott's Field recently built-over. Liverpool ferry (and from Woodside 340893) views autumn terns including some black, kittiwakes, occasional skuas (gales), moulting guillemot, gulls. See Mersey, New Brighton. A new promenade is on the upriver side of Seacombe Ferry.

Shakerley Meres. 734716. By M6. Old sand-quarries, heath, birch-alder-wood with car-park. n little and unsuccessful common ringed plovers, great crested and little grebes, Canada geese, coot, sand-martin (Sandmere), turtle-dove, lesser whitethroat. v tufted duck, goldeneye, dunlin, black-tailed godwit, black tern. Boating.

Shotton Pools (Clwyd). See Burton.

Shotwick Lake. 315723. Welsh border reservoir, restricted access steelworks Weighbridge Road from A550 Queensferry and private marsh-road from Burton Station Road-end. Yachting often disturbs waterfowl to small elevated reservoirs near railway or field-floods. v bittern Jan/80, once 3,000 duck, mallard, teal, pintail, 60 tufted, 164 pochard, goldeneye, shoveler, gadwall, occasional smew, ruddy, longtail, 3 divers, grebes including black-necked and red-necked (top reservoir Feb/79 frost); glaucous gull Nov/83; 2nd Deeside greater yellowlegs Nov/83. I saw male goosander Feb/83 and 2 grey phalaropes Oct/82. Adjacent Sealand stubble-fields: n corn-bunting, tree-sparrow, whinchat, oyster-catcher, red-legged partridge. v, especially with slurry or rain-floods: mallard, pintail, teal, etc, Bewick's and whooper swans, Russian and Greenland (Feb/84) whitefronted, pinkfoot and Canada geese; 12 spp wader including curlew, green and wood-sandpipers, ruff, little stint, black-tailed godwit, dunlin, little ringed plover, spotted redshank, short-eared owl, bittern, Feb/82, hen-harrier, hobby Sept/84, merlin, occasional buzzard, glaucous gull, raven, water-pipit, buff-breasted, pectoral, curlew and sharp-tailed sandpipers. Shotwick Dale, A550; n grey wagtail (Woodbank). See Burton. Black tern, are regular passage migrants. Nearby Weighbridge Road-Sealand Industrial Estate field pools and stubble attract golden plover, stints and other waders: Temminck's stint 1962, sharp-tailed sandpiper Sept-Oct/73, buff-breasted Oct/73, dowitcher Oct/70. A crane was on Shotwick fields Aug/86 making 136 species. A white-winged black tern Oct/81.

Stalybridge Brushes, 990010. Moorland valley-steam with reservoirs to Swineshaw; small mixed plantation, to Harridge-Hollingworth Hall moors, 980995 (red grouse). n redstart, dipper, wheatear, sandpiper, golden plover, ring-ouzel, twite, short-eared and little owls. v pied flycatcher, teal, tufted duck, scaup, merlin, occasional buzzard, Temminck's stint Arnfield resvr 9/71, cormorant.

**Stanlow Point, Gowy Estuary*. 427775; 28 ft; sandstone former island Mersey side Ship Canal, M.N.A. reserve , restricted access, shrubs. n shelduck, blackcap, etc, starling-roost; 3 miles stone causeway where the Mersey comes sparkling down to Mt Manisty, part shrubs, n occasional stonechat. v bramblings, goldfinch, linnet, snow-bunting, up to 28 twite, rock-pipit, 14,000 pintail with 25,000 duck from Mersey shooting areas Oct, peak 16,000 Nov-Jan moving, according to wind with Ince Bank. Each tide brings the sky alive with wings clouds of slender pintail, droves of teal, wigeon and mallard blacken winter tide-lines until incoming tides (15 mins later than Liverpool) when they float in rafts before us on the causeway. Pintail often remain on 3 miles muddy Stanlow-Manisty Bay in Aster, Atriplex, etc, close to causeway, between biggest tides. February passage of emigrating common gulls. v to 67 great crested grebes Dec/84; 20-100 shoveler, 80 cormorants Jan/85, Leach's petrel Sept/80. Gulls include occasional kittiwake, glaucous, Iceland. Short-eared owls, water-rail, ruff, great and arctic skuas in gales, guillemot, gannet (dead), 2,000 "commic" terns Aug-Sept, up to 178 great crested grebes Feb/86 winter here, formerly white-fronted now occasional pinkfooted geese, peregrine, merlin, grey plover, waders, goosander Oct/78. Still 186 wigeon, 35 pintail mid-April. Feeding flocks of feral and woodpigeons, stock and collared doves, occasional water-pipit, snow-bunting; goosander Oct/82; occasionally n redshank, ringed plover, yellow wagtail, shelduck, whinchat. Best concentrations of duck biggest 10 m tides with W winds sending birds from more exposed Dee. Connected by 3 miles causeway upriver to Ince Gorse (for Ince Bank) and Frodsham Score. See Mersey, Manisty, Ince. A common sandpiper wintered 1984/5. Stanlow pokes its sandstone head into the Mersey beyond the oil refineries in sudden tranquility amidst mile after windswept mile of deceivingly barren-looking marsh. The glinting smoothness of this mud conceals Macoma and Hydrobia shells, and worms, the food of thousands of waders which flock to its ebbing tides, the refuge of more winter wildfowl than any other estuary in Northwestern Europe. Hordes of slender pintail and whistling wigeon criss-cross the sky or ride with rafts of mallard along the misty edge of the marsh. In dark silhouette on a December day, a fierce little merlin flashes across as we lunch in the causeway bank, while the river echoes the mournful cries of grey plovers. It crash-lands into the Spartina and emerges dragging a skylark in its left foot, to tug and tear at its breast in full view. At other times a fleeting shadow low over the marsh comes to life in a big, brown female peregrine as wild as the weather where the incoming tide meets the relentless icy Russian blast blowing downriver.

Tabley Park & Mere. 12 ft deep, 49 acres, private, SW Knutsford, A556; SJ 716713. n lakeside heronry c 62 nests 1985, 45 after frost 1986, reed-warbler, tufted, shoveler, occasionally teal, ruddy duck, tree-creeper, nuthatch, kingfisher, woodcock, grebes, Canada geese, water-rail 1954, mute swan, rookery. v to 90 tufted duck, garganey, shoveler, cormorant, 370 coot Jan; siskin, occasional buzzard; escaped American wigeon Feb/51. Nuthatches nest commonly.

Tabley Park mere, a spring heronry and winter haunt of wildfowl.
(Photo Eric Hardy)

Tatton Park & Mere. NT; SJ 737815; 2,085 acres, off A34, B 5087, Knutsford; car park Ashley Rd from A5034, or foot-entrance King Street end. Long, shallow lake over 1 mile, 60 acres, plus Melchett Pool below Hall. Irregular opening times. Cheshire's largest public park, c 12 miles circumference; public disturbance, boating. n grebes, tufted, ruddy, occasionally teal and shoveler duck; mute swan, Canada goose, nuthatch, woodcock, kingfisher, stockdove, 3 woodpeckers, redstart, hawfinch, occasional snipe, curlew/73; 6500 woodpigeons Dec/73; a buzzard, little owl, long-tailed and willow tits, redshank, reed, sedge and garden-warblers; rookery Knutsford Lodge. v c700 Canadas from Tabley, etc, 350 tufted Aug, 160 teal, 100 pochard Dec/57, goldeneye April, 30 shoveler Aug, up to 47 great crested grebes Nov/73 occasional slavonian 50 cormorants Feb, 50 ruddy duck Oct, occasional smew, longtail, gadwall, pintail, merganser, goosander, scoter, bittern, spotted crake (Melchett Pool), water-rail, 480 winter coot, 700 swifts late May; terns including arctic, roseate May/76, black April & Aug jack snipe, black-necked grebe, buzzard, hobby July/73, great black-backed gull, great skua Nov/76, red-breasted 1984 & pied flycatchers, firecrest, water-pipit Mar/75, two-barred crossbill April/74, siskin, redwing-roost Higmere Plantation, greenshank, dunlin,oystercatcher, knot. White-winged black tern has been noted and a crane Feb/1966. A great northern diver was calling on the lake Dec/85 with buzzard and short-eared owl park visitors. Nuthatches nest and pochard used to. See Knutsford. Stockdoves and lesser spotted woodpecker nest. A Mediterranean gull visitor May/87.

Thewall. See Woolston, Lymm.

Thornton Manor Park. 3000818. Private, Leverhulme Estate. n lake islands heronry c 17n; Canada goose, sparrowhawk, garden-warbler, little grebe, nuthatch, mallard, coot, goldcrest, tree-sparrow, rookery Thornton Hough village. v tufted duck, teal, cormorant, ruddy duck. Great crested grebes nest here.

Thurstaston Common, Royden Park (Hill Bark), NT, 298 ft gorsey sandstone hill, pine-birch plantations, via Frankby 245859, Irby Mill Hill quarry 254856, School Lane footpath 248846, "Cottage Loaf" A540; 248845, etc. n sparrowhawk, redpoll, tree-creeper, nuthatch, lesser whitethroat, 3 wood-peckers, shelduck, formerly nightjar & long-eared owl. v occasional buzzard Sept/78, firecrest, woodcock, Richard's pipit Nov/82, great grey shrike, crossbill Mar/83. Dee shore, Dawpool & Cliff-fields, Station Rd end below church, 236835. Wader-roost (ringed at night), day time people disturbance; Icelandic black-tailed godwits, dunlin, oystercatcher, turnstone, etc, occasional snow-bunting, shore-lark Richard's pipit, glaucous gull, quail, Lapland bunting tip Nov/81, spoonbill July/73. Wirral Way information room. See Heswall, West Kirby. House-sparrows nest in holes in high clay cliffs Thurstaston shore. The glaucous returned to the shore for its 6th winter in Aug/86. Tree-pipits nest.

Tintwistle Reservoirs, 025973, Low Moor Heath, 750 ft twite May/Aug. See Longdendale.

Trentabank Reservoir. See Langley. An osprey was here Apr/86. 20 pairs of herons nested at its heronry 1985. Pied flycatchers use nest-boxes.

Wallasey. Canada geese, occasionally little grebe, tufted duck, heron Central Park; kestrel n St Nicholas church, house-martins Sheer Rd, Promenade; barn-owl Poulton Rd to 1978. A long-eared owl visited a Liscard garden May/73. Pied and spotted flycatchers, redstart, Greenland wheatear p.m. Rake Lane Cemetery. See New Brighton,Seacombe.

Warrington. Appleton/Walton Hall resvr 600843. n great crested and little grebes, ruddy duck, reed-warbler, etc. v. 50 tufted duck Jan, wigeon, teal, etc, black tern, once white-winged; ruff, green sandpiper, greenshank, dunlin, golden plover, spotted redshank, once red-necked phalarope, occasional Bewick's swan, buzzard, slavonian grebe Feb/86. Disturbed by angling. Water lowered some summer droughts. House-martin n Bold Street, rooks Wilson Patten Street, blackbirds central multi-storey car-park 1981, lesser spotted woodpecker Appleton Dingle and kingfishers by Ship Canal, Warburton Bridge. See Woolston; Moss Side.

**Weaver Estuary* (Bend). Via Frodsham High Street, Marsh Lane 514776, motorway-bridge & Saltport track to privilege parking up bank; also Frodsham Hill, Ship Street 517779, motorway-bridge to ICI Sludge (n little ringed plover, etc, v waders). Shallow, muddy; tide 30 mins after Liverpool; spring tides to Dutton Locks. Up to 12 autumn waders at ebb; best waterfowl long frost when gather from meres. n occasional coot, grebes (see Weston), little ringed plover. I began recording its birds 1920s and have records back to pre-Ship Canal collections local Weston Hall squire, etc. v up to 790 coot Dec/81, 539 pochard, 580 teal, 158 tufted, 500 wigeon Mar/59, 15 goldeneye, 30 shelduck, odd longtail, pintail, 24 shoveler Aug, 5 smew frost Dec/81, odd scaup, common and velvet-scoters, mergansers, occasional goosander, 17 ruddy duck, eider winter 1952/3, garganey, feral gadwall, 13 Bewick's swans, 8 bean-geese claimed Feb/84; 5 grebes include wintering flock little; Manx shearwater gale: herons. 7 American waders: pectoral, buff-breasted, white-rumped, Baird's Sept/63, Sept/75 and Sept/82, stilt (Apr-Sept/84, May/82), semi-palmated and western sandpipers; green, wood and common sandpipers, 3 phalaropes, avocet (Dec and May), stilt May/83; up to 100 little stints autumn occasional spring and over-winter; 200 curlew-sandpipers July/72, ICI sludge; least sandpiper Oct/72, godwits, spotted redshank, regular greenshank, up to 50 ruff in one of major nothern autumn winter haunts. Occasional knot, sanderling, grey plover, Temminck's stint, 120 snipe, spoonbill, marsh-harrier May, occasional hen-harrier; merlin, peregrine, short-eared owl, terns including black, occasional white-winged, and whiskered records, little July-Aug, common, arctic. Up to 12 little, occasional Sabine's, glaucous, Iceland, Mediterranean, Franklin's (Apr/84) and kittiwake (gale Oct/83) gulls. White-winged black tern Aug/81, etc; pirouetting and dipping rapidly its slender bill catching midges and maggots to build its energy reserve of fat to winter on the sea off West Africa, the little red-necked phalarope has fed here regardless of our admiring attention until the watery plume of a speed-boat and its skier scared it off. A Manx shearwater was in flight after storms Sept/83. An olive-backed pipit detailed Apr/86, Wilson's phalarope Sept/81. Marsh-harriers are fairly regular spring-autumn, red-necked phalarope (July/86) more occasional than literature implies. Best when high tide sends birds off Mersey or low water neap tides for autumn waders but regulated by Weaver sluice. Occasional aquatic warbler (Sept/75; Aug/77), snow-bunting, rock-pipit, whinchat; big autumn concentrations 300/1,000 swifts and house-martins. *Rocksavage Pool*: 522796. Private reedy, muddy willow-pool CEGB & MRG. Ringing station, Bank Road, Frodsham Bridge. Restricted access. n grasshopper, reed and sedge-warblers, stonechat 1977, v 96 spp in year; swallow-roost, 100 + snipe, water-rail, occasional spotted crake, autumn, jack snipe, Cheshire's first Cetti's warbler Apr/84, aquatic Aug/75, ruff, spotted redshank, pectoral sandpiper Aug/81, little ringed plover, water-pipit, occasional snow-bunting, teal, little gull, little stint, wood and curlew-sandpipers, occasional woodcock, etc. See Weston; Frodsham. Ospley visitor April 1987. A gull-billed tern June/87.

Weaver Sluices. 499800. Mersey tidal marsh overlooked from Frodsham Marsh Saltport bank at Weaver-ship Canal junction. v up to 4,500 teal Feb, 4,800 golden plover Mar, 4,000 dunlin, 470 pintail Dec, 800 mallard, 1,000 shelduck Dec.

Weaver Valley. 50 miles of wooded banks from Peckforton SE to Staffs border, then N via Nantwich (receives Dane), and Northwich, often with wintering green and common sandpipers, to enter Ship Canal, Frodsham. Fewer winter flood-fields now with grebes, Bewick's swan (Aston), redshank, curlew, ruff, black tern and teal since water-table lowered. Occasional overwintering little stint; up to 30 cormorants Frodsham-Dutton in frost Feb/85. n marsh-tit, 3 woodpeckers, sandpiper, etc Footpaths upriver from Frodsham swing-bridge 535788 to Dutton Flashes, and from Overton, 526776, to Kingsley Pools. Frodsham Weir reed-bed: n reed, grasshopper and sedge-warblers, v purple heron Sept/79, snipe. Sand-martins occasionally n above Frodsham. See Kingsley. Little grebes at Nantwich. In the big frost in February 1986, up to 19 cormorants roosted in trees near Pickering's Lock above Frodsham, where smaller numbers roost in winter. Grey wagtail, little grebe, n Nantwich.

West Kirby. The gate to the Dee mouth. 210868, bottom of Dee Lane with car-parking and access to Hilbre via Little Eye 3 hrs before HW, and to LW Tanskey Rocks, 205865 for autumn-winter brent feeding on emerald enteromorphous algae, up to 50 wigeon, shelduck, etc. Shore to Hoylake Red Rocks for HW autumn-winter wader-roosts (disturbed by dog-owners and horse-riders) with up to 4/10,000 oystercatchers Oct, 2,000 Jan, to 5,000 dunlin, knot, redshank, 500 Aug sanderling, 120 grey plover Sept, godwits, ringed and ocasional Kentish plover on ebb, occasional curlew-sandpiper. White wagtails (March-April); occasional brent and snow-bunting; rarely shore-lark. When not disturbed by weekend boats, the Marine Lake below Dee Lane has had up to 40 goldeneye, 12 mergansers, occasional scaup, scoter, longtail (I saw 4 wintering 1936-7, male in full plumage to May 20), velvet-scoter (I flushed first two, Nov/32), tufted duck and pochard (Jan frost); great crested, little (frost) and black-necked (Sept/36, etc) grebes; black-throat diver, cormorants, occasionally shag and grey phalarope. It has declined recently but has waders when drained. House-martin n Raeburn Avenue, etc. A bittern visited the reserve pool Gilroy Road end of municipal golf-course Jan/85. See Hoylake, Caldy, Wirral Way. Plans to enlarge the marine lake will increase boating disturbance and reduce the area of tidal wader-roosts. Stapledon Wood, Caldy is a minor bird-haunt, with nesting nuthatch, great and lesser spotted woodpeckers.

Weston Marsh. 510795. 69½ acres, formerly tidal marsh and Cheshire's largest island, now tethered by Rocksavage Causeway,

Weaver Estuary. In 1954 I negotiated for MNA with Manchester Ship Canal the first Mersey Estuary wildfowl-reserve here, continuing after ICI purchase until their industrial tip raised level above tide, 1970. No access, but viewed from opposite bank of Weaver, Frodsham Marsh. Up to 4,000 golden plover roost; v short-eared owl, occasional tawny pipit (1984) with 25 spp shore-waders visiting Weaver bank, including godwits, ruff, stints, occasional avocet, etc. n corn-bunting, lapwing, occasional grebes, coot, tufted duck in "The Rushes", often flooded-out by tide.

Whitegate Way. 605692. See Delamere.

Wildboarclough. 983688. See East; Bosley.

Winsford Bottom Flash. 657655. The "Cheshire Broads", 2 miles, 12-18 ft deep, boating, angling. n great crested and little grebes, reed-warbler, mute swan, occasional feral shelduck. v up to 230 coot Jan, 250 pochard, 225 tufted, 138 wigeon, 88 mallard, 60 ruddy duck, 20 teal, 8 goosander, 3 goldeneye, 40 cormorants (Feb), herons, occasional whooper and Bewick's swans, longtailed duck.

Wirral Way. Old railway-footpath, 1st half shrubby from Hooton Station Bridge 349783 to Neston with road-diversion Leahurst; more open West Kirby Grange Road 215869 to Parkgate with n grasshopper-warbler, Caldy, Neston; sparrowhawk Caldy; lesser whitethroat Parkgate, Neston, etc. v hen-harrier Gayton; marsh-tit, redwings, fieldfares, waxwing. The Wirral Way was conceived in the committee of MNA, to turn the old Wirral Railway into a linear country-park. As our president, the late P.G. Garlick, was also chairman of Wirral Green Belt Council, we handed all Wirral conservation, including this project to them and they pursued the matter with Cheshire County Council who established it in 1969. Waxwing, great grey shrike and firecrest at Parkgate, hen-harrier and short-eared owl at Heswall-Gayton golf-course, and nesting grasshopper-warbler, Caldy-Neston, were listed in our preliminary report published by WCBG, 1966.

Withington (Lower) SF. 813698. Lancashire border. n sand-martin. declining; Canada goose, tufted duck, marsh-tit, turtle-dove, occasional corn-bunting. v goldeneye, pochard, ruff, scoter, dunlin, records of firecrest, long-billed dowitcher Aug/64, jack snipe, little crake, water-rail, marsh-harrier, black-tailed godwit in its better days. Sandpits have winter duck.

Woodside Ferry, Birkenhead. Terns, occasional lauks, Caspian tern claimed Sept/75 gull-size, very red bill, dark under primaries.

**Woolston Weir-Thelwell Eyes*. 340 acres reedy, willowy, non-tidal peninsula, Mersey-Ship Canal reserve. Restricted access via Latchford Lock, Warrington on A50 at 628871 or Weir Lane, Woolston towpath, 656888; permits from sec, 45 Albert Rd,

Grappenhall, Warrington or Latchford Lock. 186 spp including international status and 3rd-12th British Counts for teal to 4,590 Jan/82 frost, 7th for shoveler to 566 Sept. 54 n include great crested and little grebes, shoveler, gadwall, pochard, teal, tufted, ruddy, occasional shelduck; sand-martin, reed, sedge and grasshopper-warblers, reed-bunting, stonechat, meadow-pipit, yellow wagtail, black-headed gulls, mute swan, Canada goose, redshank, little ringed plover, common ringed plover, oystercatcher, lesser whitethroat, long-tailed tit, bullfinch etc. v include 1,470 pochard March, 770 mallard, 211 tufted, Dec, 782 pintail Feb, 152 ruddy, 36 gadwall Oct, goldeneye, wigeon, garganey, (has summered, like pintail) goosander, 480 coot Aug, occasional geese including pinkfeet flights Jan/85 frost, Bewick's swan Feb-March, marsh and hen-harriers, occasional hobby, black-necked grebe, black terns, 60 ruff Sept/80, 60 dunlin, 16 ringed plover; green, common, occasionally wood and buff-breasted (July/84) sandpipers, greenshank, curlew, spotted, redshank, avocet May, 500 snipe Nov frost, golden plover, little stint, curlew-sandpiper, occasional sanderling, turnstone, woodcock, smew, scaup, up to 4 short-eared owls; little (May/81), Franklin's Apr/84 and glaucous gulls, whiskered tern June/83, water-rail, beared tit May/81, Dec/77. Passerine moulting area, especially willow and blue tits; swallow-roost Aug-Sept; corn-bunting and late summer starling roosts. Ortolan bunting and crossbill were added Oct/86 when 250 shoveler were there. Two Temminck's stints and a white-winged black tern were there 13 July 1986. Little gull and pintail have summered. A storm-petrel was blown in Sept/80. A laughing gull was at Latchford Locks Oct/86, Savi's warbler June/85, 7 little gulls May/85, also 232 snipe in February and occasional visits of avocet, white-rumped sandpiper, rough-legged buzzard, water-pipit, snow-bunting and great skua. A record count of 1700 pochard with 220 tufted duck was made in the big frost March, 1986 while 1800 were still at Rostherne. White-winged black tern, Temminck's stint and black-necked grebe June-July/86. 31 black terns and a gale-blown arctic skua made record days in September 1986. A spoonbill, Apr/87.

Wybunbury Moss. 701502. NCC. Restricted. 26 acres, 2 miles S of Crewe, access near old church tower and Moss Lane. Floating, shrubby, rush and reed peat-bog with birch-pine wood. 106 spp. n include 3 woodpeckers, red-legged partridge, grasshopper, garden and reed-warblers,lesser whitethroat, turtle-dove, stockdove, corn-bunting, marsh, long-tailed and willow tits, sparrowhawk, little owl, water-tail, snipe, curlew, goldcrest, yellow wagtail, tree-sparrow, tree-creeper, nuthatch. v firecrest, siskin, woodcock. Sand-quarry pool: occasional goosander, black-necked grebe Feb/85.

Specially Interesting Birds

Not all records are sent to local Reports or the National Rarities Committee. Unconfirmed and critical claims will always be disputed as Cheshire has no unanimous, completely representative authority. 328 species and 8 subspecies have been recorded wild, as well as 35 alien escapes and introductions. 130 species nest or have nested here. However, the *rara avis* is not our only interest. To many the kingfisher's flash of blue, the sight of sanderling chasing the tide's edge like silver birds, or the long-winged harrier's lazy flight are a welcome novelty. I have selected some of the characteristic birds which have special county interests or enrich the experience of distant visitors.

Great Crested Grebe. Cheshire shares with Norfolk three-quarters of Britain's breeding population, nesting on over 50 waters from Moreton brickworks at the coast to Bosley Mere and Radnor reservoir in the eastern hills, south to Sandbach and Alsager Mere, occasionally the Dee steelworks-pools, Frodsham sludgebed 1971, and the Weaver Estuary, (1941) with 10 pairs at Rostherne Mere 1982. Occasionally it rears a third brood. Never did Quixote pursue a more chivalrous romance than that of these imaculate birds, head-shaking on every mere sparkling in spring sunshine. Boating precludes them from nesting on some waters like Shotwick Lake and Pickmere where they bred in 1884. Anglers stocking waters with fish doubled their haunts since early this century as I described in a paper in Salmon & Trout Association Mag., No 139, 1953. They colonised Lymm Dam 1901, Astle Pool in the south in 1912, Baddiley 1919, Northwich Flashes 1924 and Hatchmere 1931, Thornton Manor 1984. Larger flocks winter offshore, Sept-May especially in hard frosts, with 100-300 off Hilbre, HW off Leasowe, New Brighton, up to 178 Feb/86 on the Mersey off Stanlow and Eastham, over 20 on the Dee off Heswall, and on the Weaver Estuary. I have seen odd ones on the Ship Canal. On 1 Oct/62 I described in the Liverpool Daily Post discovering the stomachs of great crested grebes (from Cheshire) which died in oil-pollution along the North Wales coast, crammed with bright green grass-like enteromorphous algae and no feathers, or fish, the first evidence that they changed their diet to this at sea though 15% of their mainly fishy diet on freshwater is vegetation. Spring assemblies of 20-70 are usually found on such meres as Marbury Park, Rostherne, Tatton, Doddington, Combermere, Barmere, etc. One r Lincolnshire reached Cheshire. Little grebes nest widespread wherever reedy pools are deep enough, even Wirral's Rabymere, and small flocks wintering on the Weaver Estuary and Dee steelworks-pools increase greatly in frost. Black-necked grebes have bred at Rostherne 1939, Oakmere Arm, 1941 & 1953, Abbots Moss 1942 and Nunsmere 1984 but seldom persist and

The nightjar, an almost extinct Cheshire bird, formerly nested on most heaths from Wirral to Delamere and eastern cloughs. (Photo C.F. Mayos)

are better known as winter visitors, like the slavonian and red-necked grebes on both Mersey and Dee and occasionally inland. The latter is the scarcest and here chiefly when the Baltic is frozen in hard weather. Grebes distribute parasites of fishes. Grebes have wintered on the Mersey for a long time. Mather the Liverpool taxidermist had several including black-necked fron the Mersey in winter, and Squire Banks shot one at Weston in the Weaver estuary in pre-canal 1854. In 1986, 8 pairs nesting at Rostherne reared only 1 young due to predation by mink. A Slav grebe on Shotwick Lake Dec/86.

Grey Heron. Spreading its enormous wings to beat its weary-looking way, flying slowly like a blown rag, across the sky, the heron is a common sight. A chattering of young herons marks a dozen woods early in Spring.

Standing like a sentry or stalking the waterside in stately steps, the lanky heron is usually met in lonely lakeside vigil; but up to 40 may stand silver-grey around the Weaver-Frodsham marshes in spring and autumn up to 28 on Manisty shore and up to 30 by the Dee. Others roost at Witton flashes, raid suburban goldfish-ponds in early morning, sometimes fish Birkenhead Park lake, frequently visit Hilbre and cross the Mersey estuary in autumn. Like the bittern, they distribute parasites of fish. In their very predatory diet I've seen them stabbing water-rails flooded out of Parkgate Spartina shore by HW, and in British Birds magazine July/78 I described finding young grey squirrels in food-pellets at Combermere heronry, One has taken two fish with one stroke.

So many fish-waters are again responsible for the 2nd to 4th largest population in the country, probably naming Chester's Handbridge (Heronbridge) and Rostherne (roost of the Heron). Heronries of 30/40 n Eaton Park Duckwood, by the Dee; 40/70 Tabley Mere; 30/48 Combermere Great Wood; c 10 tormented by a rookery at Keckwickford Green Wood, Moore; c16 Thornton Manor lake islands c12 Langley; c4 Radnor; a few Marbury Park Mere, Oakmere pines (none 1984), 5 private Rode Hall, Rode Heath. An increase from 5, including Eaton & Tabley, noted in 1871 by Yarrell. Odd n have been built in recent years Burton, Ledsham Inglewood, Fernilees, Kingsley's Devil's Gardens, Aston Long Acre, Longdendale, Sandbach, Cholmondeley Park etc. Nesting is often reduced or ended by tree-felling or severe winters. Young birds nesting at Moore dispersed N to Furness, Ireland, South Wales the Midlands, Cumbria and Durham; and to East Anglia, Devon and Denbighshire, while those from Eaton (Chester) went to the Midlands and Severn Estuary. Birds r in Birkenhead, Bedfordshire and Shropshire came to the Weaver Estuary and from Staffordshire to the Gowy. An Oslo-ringed bird was found in Birkenhead docks in autumn 1939 and one from Gloucestershire visited Hazelgrove, Stockport. Another ringed at Staffordshire's Gailey Pool wintered in Wallasey Central Park. Four or five pairs from the Moore heronry began nesting in recent years in field-trees at Keckwickford Corner by the Daresbury Road. A few nest at Trentabank reservoir, Langley, east Cheshire.

I have seen the darker purple heron on the Dee steelworks-marshes, Sept/61, and another was off Parkgate Dec/70. Winter bitterns, probably from the continent (as a fowler told me one he flushed off Parkgate and drove across the Dee to shoot it over the Welsh border outside the old Cheshire bird-law's protection, was r in Saxony), are irregular visitors to Rostherne, Tatton, Frodsham Marsh, Neston shore-reeds, Cholmondeley and Lymm. One r in Norfolk was recovered at Alderley Edge. In April/84 I was given a little bittern found dead in Eastham Locks of the Ship Canal. Others at Birkenhead May/69 and Frodsham Marsh Aug/70. A night heron at Moore May/62 may have escaped from a Scottish zoo.

Geese. Some 2,000 loud-voiced Canadians graze country parks and splash down on meres, the larger flocks at Tabley, Tatton, Rostherne, Cholmondeley and Barmere; smaller ones at Doddington, Thornton Manor, Wallasey Central Park, with evidence of some making late summer moult-migrations to Yorkshire. Many n. in Eaton Park graze Churton-Aldford meadows and there is some movement from the Midlands. Occasional hybrids and smaller escaped varieties add to the confusion. Feral greylags are the next noisy nuisance, some 30 cackling around Eaton, 40/80 at Cholmondelry Mere, some 30 moulting on Rostherne, and others occasionally visiting the Weaver-Mersey and other waters, to the confusion of our wildfowl-surveys. The original Cheshire wild geese, Russian white-fronted which came with pinkfeet when the Dee marshes were reclaimed below Puddington and Sealand, declined when overshot (Shooting Times 18/2/39). The pinkfeet flock moved to south Lancashire mossland potato-farms about 1928; but since their massive increase there in recent years, surplus birds have since 1979 increasingly visited Dee and Mersey, especially in hard winters. Whitefronts, which wintered by Aldford Meadows until there were drained, and roosted on the Mersey off Ince Gorse, moved to the Montgomeryshire Severn in 1940s and are frequently seen gabbling over mid-south Cheshire in flight to those haunts. A few with occasional Greenlanders visit Shotwick fields and Burton marshes. One has found fowlers so confused over goose-identification, calling almost anything "brants" or "blue geese", even Canadas "barnacles" that little support can be given to historic claims of a former abundance of barnacles on the Dee. Odd barnacles frequently appearing on inland waters, even a flock by the Mersey at Frodsham Dec/80, are escapes from waterfowl-collections. In 1955 we received ambitious press-handouts from Dee wildfowlers claiming big flocks of brent were soon to return after their introduction of eel-grass (Zostera). The Dee still has only its usual few autumn-winter visitors from Hilbre to Burton, mostly dark-bellied, occasionally the light form, and the last Zostera was still that at Hoylake, 1851. A flock of yelping pinkfeet fed regularly on a friend's farm between Kingsley and Norley in the big frost in 1979, and a few visit Rostherne. I came upon odd snow-geese (Eaton), bean, bar-headed, even pinks, hybrid lesser whitefront and other exotics from collections which are best forgotten. Cheshire is fast becoming like Norfolk, a farmyard-overflow of feral waterfowl which should be culled in the interest of scientific field-work.

The Cheshire Swan

The Swallow flies fast, but remember
The Swallow with summer is gone.
What Bird is their left in November
To rival the Tarporley Swan?

There's no longer a regatta of 100 swans patrolling the Dee at Chester Groves, the Weaver at Frodsham Bridge or Northwich, or the meres, to meet Egerton-Warburton's poem. Once with one of the three densest populations in Britain, Cheshire's mute swans declined to some 10 breeding pairs with more non-breeders. Again the product of its many meres, the Cheshire Swan is the introduced mute swan, the white swan badge of the Cheshire Hunt, giving its name to Tarporley's Swan Inn since 1762 and Swan Green near Peover. 12/20 are a large herd nowadays though formerly the musical wings of an immpressive frost-flight of 24 attracted my attention over Frodsham marsh. Its chief haunts are Doddington, Winsford, Combermere, Radnor, Sandbach, Eaton Serpentine, Langley, Frodsham pumping

The Cheshire swan. A pair of mute swans, recovering slowly from their recent decline attributed to lead poisoning from anglers' weights, gunshot or lead boat-paint, and the loss of underwater food-plants. (Photo A. Woodgate)

pools with winter herds on Shotwick Lake, occasional frost visitors to West Kirby ML: three visited Hilbre July/84, and continued to North Wales; Birkenhead Docks, Hoylake shore and the Dee marshes, where a pair nested unsuccessfully recently. Vandalism contributed to their demise in Birkenhead and other town parks; others bungled into overhead wires. Despite recent lead-poisoning from anglers' weights and gunshot-pellets grubbed up for grit, Doddington's pre-war herd of up to 150 was decimated by cestode worm haemorrhage disease in 1932, probably due to overpopulation reducing food. Ringing found movements with Shropshire, Berkshire, Staffordshire, Montgomeryshire, Warwickshire, Holyhead and Barrow dock (probably for moulting), and between Liverpool parks and Frodsham, Dee and Weaver, Barmouth and Dee. In March 1986 the cob of a pair on the Weaver Estuary attacked and killed a rival mute swan. The earliest record is 1387, in the "Compotus Rool" of Newhall Manor, Aston.

In contrast, wild swans continue to increase, especially spring migration herds of Bewick's swans along the coast and at Liverpool Bay Bar Light, on Mersey, Dee and Weaver as well as the meres. A great chevron of 44 in bugling chorus flew over us one March evening as we left Marbury Park Mere, carrying on over the Mersey. Some winter on the Dee marshes in hard winters and visit Shotwick fields. The present large wintering Ribble herd began in the 1960s visiting Ince Bank in smaller numbers, before changing its winter feeding territory. A few whoopers visit Dee and Mersey chiefly and feral birds from Lancashire's Martin Mere visited Sandbach in summer. Fuelled by fat-reserves and urged on by shortening daylight, Bewick's swans, tireless voyagers from the Karal Sea come 2000 miles from the Siberian Arctic in long waving lines of marble white wings with haunting, fluting cries. Guided through the night like the larger whooper by Polaris and the constellation Cygnus, The Swan or Northern Cross stretching its mythical wings down the Milky Way in the star-cluttered sky, they increase annually at their major haunts in neighbouring Lancashire. I have seen them migrating by night as well as day in March, over mid-Cheshire and the Wirral sea.

Shelduck. Two great estuaries with miles of mud, the Dee teeming with Hydrobia shellfish food, the Mersey with Macoma, and their wooded banks, assure a great population of international status. The Mersey, averaging 7.3% of W.European counts, reached its record 12,170 in Nov/81, second to The Wash nationally. The Dee had 7,315 off Parkgate-Heswall Oct/80, third in Britain. Although occasionally nesting in holes in Frodsham Score, Stanlow Point, the Dee Training Wall and steelworks, Woolston, Manistry, Middle Hilbre, Rocksavage, Weaver Estuary, Weston Marsh, Clifton, Wallasey and Hoylake golf-dunes, most breed in woods like Burton, Denhall, Haddon Wood, Thurstaston-Royden Park, Heswall, Willaston, Caldy, Meols, Shotwick, Norton Priory, Walton and Moore. Post-war industrialisation and urbanisation caused a marked decline in NW Wirral. As well as ruddy shelduck escapes, common shelduck from private collections breed inland, occasionally at Doddington, Sandbach, Winsford, Oakmere, Combermere, Nantwich/84 etc. The M.N.A.'s 13 years' annual 1957 /71 breeding census counted up to 1,130 adults and 93 y on the Dee and 162 ad with 93 y on the Mersey. Many are non-breeders; occasionally shelduck nest below Fiddlers Ferry.

Pre-moult flocks gather off Heswall-Parkgate; Hilbre spring flocks may reach 350, and others may be seen off New Brighton. One can see the heavy July and August evening moult-migration flocks strung goose-like across the sky from 7-30 to 10 pm, labouring in humpbacked flight inland above Neston, Eastham or the Weaver, maybe with North Wales' birds, deflected NE by industrial chimneys along the flight-line via Weston, Runcorn Heath, Dutton, Moss-Side, Thelwall-Woolston, Stretton, Heaton Mersey, East Cheadle,

Curlew, a nesting bird of the east Cheshire moors and occasional the central plain. (Photo C.F. Mayos)

Sinderland, Ringway (or Sandbach), Goyt, Tintwistle and Longdendale until lost as they climb higher in gathering dusk. M.N.A.'s 22 years' annual moult-migration survey 1950/71 had up to 300 sightings in evenings, with wide gaps between flights, an average 88% of the population, 2,030 in 80 flights June 9-August 7 under cloudless skies, over 1,000 from Parkgate and over 1,793 in 56 flights past Weston. Returning birds, Sept-Dec, appear on inland waters like Rostherne, Combermere and Sandbach, and though 4,300 were already back on the Dee off Heswall early in Oct/84, up to 75 remain to moult on the Dee, apart from foster parents with creches of young and 30-100 on the Mersey. Early evening circling flights of immature with incomplete chest-gorgets can be confused for moult-migration. In "*Mersey*" (Dock Board magazine), Spring 1933, before moult-migration was known, I wrote of local shelduck: "There is some migration to the Continent. British born shelduck have been taken in N.W.Germany. Autumn-ringed shelduck from the German North Sea have been taken in Lancashire."

Teal. With the pintail, this little duck put the Mersey's mile-wide glistening mud-banks on the international map when it produced annually the biggest estuarine counts, 4-11% of NW Europe, despite some temporary decline 1983 through erosion of south side feeding banks by a shifting channel which later moved north again. A peak of 35,000 were counted in Dec/81. The Dee improved to 10th national place with 3,815 Jan/84 and Woolston to 12th with 4,590 in Jan/83. At high water, the Mersey sky echoes their creeking cries. 1,000 were at Rostherne in frost, in Parkgate-Heswall shore-gutter and on Denhall Marsh Lane Dee-pools; 100-500 visit Sandbach Elton Flash, Weaver Estuary, Alford-Eaton floods, Burton's Dee rifle-pools, Moss Side, Radnor, Doddington, Combermere, Runcorn Astmoor, etc. Small flocks resort to the Dee steel-pools, Ledsham Inglewood, Burton Mere; Hilbre and the Rock Channel in gales and frost. In Jan/70, 2,755 were on 17 sites. We have found irregular nestings at Burton-Puddington marshes, Dee steel-pools, Woolston, Frodsham Marsh, Ledsham Inglewood, etc. Ringing shows Mersey teal originate so far as the Pechora and Karelia in Siberian Europe, and continue to Ireland. American blue and green-winged, and occasionally Baikal teals escaped from waterfowl-collections so often that they should not be regarded wild until proven. Our other wild teal, the summer garganey, visits the Weaver estuary and Dee and Woolston marshes chiefly. It first nested in Cheshire in 1959 at Halton Moss, since drained. Up to 1000 winter on the Mersey marsh below Fiddlers Ferry Power Station, up to 450 Shotwick Lake.

Pintail. Nowhere else in Britain do pintail pattern the sky as on the Mersey where the international record count of 18,450 was made in Nov/80, the Anglo-Welsh Dee coming second with 11,265 Nov/83 during a temporary erosion of south Mersey banks. The Mersey averages 11.3-16.5% of N.W.Europe estuarine counts and increased greatly from our prewar counts of only 1,000. Rostherne has had up to 426 in February, but here and at Sandbach Elton Flash there has recently been some decline. Flocks also visit Woolston, Aldford-Eaton floods, and smaller numbers Huntington, Radnor, Rode Pool, Doddington, Eaton Oxbow, Weaver Estuary, Marbury Park, Astmoor, Runcorn Sands and Tatton. Early birds appear in August and odd ones sometimes over summer. A pair hatched young on Frodsham old sludge-beds 1967 and 1969. Ringing recorded w.v. to the Mersey from Iceland and Russia via Germany, and to the Dee from Holland, Latvia, Estonia and the Volga Estuary. Hybrids with garganey and Bahama teal occasionally escape from collections to Weaver, etc. A few pintail visit Fiddlers Ferry lagoons in winter.

Wigeon. Whistling wildly over the green refuge of our estuaries, these immaculate duck, dressed by the birds' top tailors, are the real Mersey Sound where they provide the 6th largest British winter counts. Our earliest record of Mersey wildfowl numbers, the original Hale Hall Duck-Decoy nettings and game-book shootings, in my possession, show from 1801-1814 they took 57% "teals", 37% mallard (recorded then as "wild duck", mallard meaning male duck), 5.4% "wigeons" and the odd pintail. The river's present percentage is 39% teal, 20% pintail, 17% wigeon, 13.3% shelduck, and mallard hardly 10%. The decline in mallard was due largely to the agricultural drainage of Lancashire mossland fens where many bred. Mallard and teal are the most numerous late Neolithic duck-bones in post-glacial remains excavated by friends in the Upper Mersey Valley, Derbyshire border, described in a paper published in M.N.A.'s 1960 *NW Bird Report*. Mersey wigeon reached internationally important numbers with 0.6%-1.9% of Western Europe and up to 15,202 breaking the horizon over Ince and Stanlow banks in Dec/80. In 1983-4 the Mersey was ahead of the Ribble, averaging 9,788, but usually follows it. Ince Bank alone often has 3,000. The Dee is far behind, with only 1,500-3000. Several hundred are sometimes on the Alford-Eaton floods, up to 150 in Eaton Park, 50 to 1,000 in the Dee mouth at Tanskey Rocks near Hilbre, up to 200 at the Dee steel-pools and Denhall Pools, up to 235 Sandbach, 157 Rostherne, 140 Doddington, 160-300 Barmere, 200 Baddiley Mere, a few on Shotwick Lake, Little Marbury, Radnor, Moss Side, occasionally West Kirby M.L. Up to 500 have been in the Weaver estuary and 2,000 early one frosty morning Jan/62. Ringed birds came from Finland and Iceland to the Dee. Mersey flocks feed on *Puccinellia maritina,* sea meadow grass on Ince Bank and roost there, small flocks winter on Fiddlers Ferry lagoons and Shotwick Lake.

There is a movement from the Mersey up the Weaver to the meres; but the first arrive August-September from the East. At 7 p.m. on 28 Mar/59 700 were seen flying in 4 waves S.E. over Weston from the Weaver estuary like an emigration, similar to an incident in April 1952. Strong N.E. winds in late March's cold spell had then held up migration until 2nd April; then they changed to light N-NW, and a few days later S. Early in the evening of the 2nd April, 16 to 20 flights averaging 80 with a maximum of 400, and a total movement of 2,000 departed from the Mersey-Frodsham marshes E and SE. A count there a few days later had decreased 93%. Odd wigeon have tarried at Frodsham and on the Dee into May, sometimes summering. American wigeon visiting Tabley, Frodsham, etc were escapes from several collections, wecomed usually only by list-tickers.

Ruddy Duck. With little ringed plover and collared dove, the success story in newcomers to Cheshire, joining Canada goose, mute swan, little owl and pheasant among alien introductions to establish breeding populations. Still increasing, with 4th largest British population. It colonised the county from Staffordshire-Shropshire, and there is some winter movement between these waters and possibly the West Country. This colourful, white-cheeked little diver (sometimes confused with the red-headed immature smew in winter) nests on a score of waters with over 200 flocking in winter, up to 164 the 5th national highest Nov/83 at Combermere, 60 at Rostherne in frosts, 50 Tatton, Farmwood Pool & Radnor, over 20 Winsford Bottom, and others at Barmere, Cholmondeley, Marbury, Redesmere, Appleton, Baddiley, Quoisley, Rode Pool, Sandbach, Knutsford Mere, Kingsley, Eaton Oxbow, Dee steel-pools and in frost v the Weaver Estuary, Moreton Flash, Thornton Manor, 105

Female stonechat at nest, an occasional nester Frodsham marshes.
(Photo Dennis Green)

were on Farmwood Pool Dec/85. Ruddy duck nest at Woolston Eyes, Budworth, Nunsmere, Winsford Flashes, Combermere, Barmere, Quoisley, Baddiley, South Marbury, Radnor, Astle Pool, Redesmere, Tatton Park, Sandbach, etc. In the great frost, February 1986, 128 ruddy duck frozen off the meres, were on the Ship Canal between Lymm and Rixton, for the first time.

Hen Harrier. Although p.m. used to be shot on Burton-Parkgate marshes of the Dee, and regularly visited Thewall Eye-Woolston and Walton old sludge-bed by the Mersey, this long-winged, low-flying marsh-hawk began wintering regularly on the Dee when extensive Spartina beds increased rats, voles and other prey. Up to 7 roost in winter on the marsh opposite Parkgate car-park. One may sometimes be seen hang-gliding over the tassellated reed-tops or hunting Thurstaston-Gayton fields from the Wirral Way or below Heswall. An orange wing-tab identified an Orkney-bred visitor,(a Dutch-ringed young bird visited neighbouring Lancashire), but birds breed in North Wales, and across the East border on Goldsitch-Coombs Moss (Derbyshire), and visit Crag Hall, etc, moors. One will sometimes follow a hunting fox for prey disturbed. The summer marsh-harrier is a spring and autumn p.m., chiefly to Woolston, Frodsham Marsh and the Dee, and Montagu's less often. For 3 days in June/80,a female joined a cock Montagu's already on the Dee marshes near Burton and was observed roosting and in aerial display before it left. No details were supplied, or asked for in the incomplete recording of Cheshire birds, and for security publicity was withheld until after it left its roost.

The Cheshire Partridge. This reddish-brown variety, called *montana* the "Cheshire Partridge" in Latham's old History of Birds, (from Bullock's Liverpool collection), is only a chestnut colour-aberration, not distinctive of the county. It still occurs occasionally (Frodsham 1980). Game-preservers introduced some Hungarian stock prewar. In a late season at High Legh a pair had 9 newly hatched chicks so late as Sept 2, 1958, when pheasant-chicks hatched on August 24. I found a clutch at Frodsham on 12 Aug/80. Formerly bred annually on Mount Manisty. Red-legged partridge and hybrids with chukor are frequently introduced by game-preservers, but seldom survive many wet winters without re-introductions; Manley, Alvanley, Woolston Oct/71, Frodsham, Dee Steelworks, Puddington, Doddington, Lower Withington, etc. Quail, more often heard than seen in clover and barley-fields, are frequent summer visitors to Willaston, Ness, Denhall, Shotwick, Frodsham, Macclesfield, etc.

Oystercatcher. "Cockle-catcher" on the Dee! Like the city typist no good at any figures except her own, the eye-catching appeal of their most decorative of flights in startling black and white, with blood-orange bills and most musical of calls, the wild piping of their piccolo notes, attracts admiring attention. A furore of opposition met the local sea-fisheries Committee's 1954 desire to control their increasing predation upon young cockles. As a member of its oystercatcher sub-committee, I found no such opposition to shoots of less numerous carrion-crows in a national bird-protection society's HQ sanctuary. The population is linked to the cockle-population. After the big 1962/3 frost decimated the cocklebeds, several began daily flighting to feed inland in Wirral fields. I found earthworms, Noctuid moth and crane-fly larvae in birds shot feeding above Neston. They occasionally take sand-eels in the estuary and one winter daily flights were noted from the Dee inland to bathe in field-floods at Barnston.

Up to 10 pairs nest irregularly on Burton marshes Dee Training Wall, and steelworks, others in Shotwick fields, Manisty shore, Ship Canal Causeway, Ince 1936, Frodsham Score (1984), Walton old sludge 1970, ploughed field Weston 1958, Rocksavage, Mersey above Runcorn, Heswall, inland Ashley, Tatton and Manchester airport, while singles and pairs are frequently inland. Ringing shows winter visitors come annually from the Scottish isles and Highlands, Faroes, and Norway. With up to 42,505 Jan/82, the Dee is second only to Morecombe Bay for autumn-winter flocks passing in pied processions below Neston Fisherman's Path before rising tides. Tidal roosting including up to 13,000 off Heswall Feb; 12,000 Hilbre Oct; 10,000 Denhall-Neston gutter Jan, and Hoylake Red Rocks Jan, 6,500 roosting on Middle Hilbre Feb/56 and up to 800 inland on Bidston Moss in March, chiefly night tides. Lack of cockle and mussel food on the Mersey keeps numbers down to 10-30, with no conspicuous flocks. Albinistic and leucistic (fawn) birds are frequent On 1/3/42 I found the pointed-billed worm eating "subspecies" *ostralegus* dead at Hilbre, and on 30/3/41 an intermediate specimen.

Little Ringed Plover. First appearing as a September passage-migrant at old Altrincham sewage-beds in 1946, this successful colonist began nesting annually from 1954 near Sandiway. Its single call became a regular sound at Frodsham sludge-beds and now over 20 pairs nest annually, including Frodsham ICI sludge, Sandbach Elton, etc flashes, Chelford, Northwich Witton, Brokery Cross A599, Butterfinch Bridge-Marbury lane and flashes, Saltersley, Hog's Back Lane Quarry Delamere, though its former Plumley Ascol Lane haunt became too over-grown. It has bred at times at Nunsmere (Delamere), Rocksavage, Kingsley, Astmoor old sewagebeds, Ellesmere Port Shell compound, Lostock Gralam and Dee steel pools. From early March to early October, particulary in July, this longer-winged, really "little" plover is seen regularly on passage at the Weaver estuary where over 20 adults and young have been noted, also at Mersey Frodsham and Burton marshes, Shotwick, Sandbach, Hilbre, etc. Ringed birds have been traced from Spain to Chelford, Plumley to France and others to North Africa. Common ringed plover nests occasionally at Leasowe (1984), Woolston, Mersey, Dee and Frodsham marshes, etc. With winter counts to 100 on the Dee, it has a marked autumn passage with 500 on Ince Bank 9/61, up to 480 at the Weaver Estuary and 300 Burton in Aug and over 100 Neston marshes, 160 at Dee steel-pools in June, over 40 at Woolston, also at Red Rocks, Huntington, Sandbach, and small numbers at many inland waters. The rarer, dark-legged Kentish plover was first identified at Marbury July/1909 then on Burton marsh 2/10/49 and one visited Hoylake-West Kirby shore for 6 successive winters from 1973.

Golden Plover. Up to 4,000-5,000 wintering birds on the Mersey at Ince and the Weaver-Bend-Frodsham No 1 sludge — Western Marsh began to build up by 1950, when new sludge-beds were added at Frodsham Marsh. Their numbers qualify national importance. Many are the brighter, northern subspecies in spectacular plumage before April departure. Large flocks also winter near Wettenhall, Wardle, Hale, Fiddlers Ferry, Byerley, Ringway Airport, M56 Ashley, Shotwick-Denhall marshes, Bartington Common, Mobberley, Warford, Greasby-Saughall Massey lane-end, Allerstock, Storeton, Moss-side, etc. Nests on East moors usually over 1,000 f+. Unproven claims for the American lesser golden plover have been made.

Purple Sandpiper. Below Hilbre's old lifeboat shed, October-May, is the major NW wintering haunt of this dark, confiding wader with up to 100, especially in hard winters, most probably from Greenland and Iceland. Singles sometimes appear in August and September, even June/68 and July/70. Visitors used to confuse yellow-legged young knot. Elsewhere, up to 10 may be seen at times at New Brighton Perch Rock-Lighthouse, and when New Brighton marine-lake is emptied for cleaning. Occasionally singles along the Mersey shore to Magazine Lane and the Wirral coast to Leasowe-Meols. Odd ones have been noted on the Mersey at Ince-Stanlow in August. The recent book on Bardsey notes arrivals nearly a month earlier than Hilbre

Ruff. Despite a decline in the Weaver Estuary-Frodsham Marsh area since this was one of Britain's 3 major wintering grounds of Russian birds, with 500+ Jan/77 and 70+ Sept/80, still outstanding passage-haunt with males, sometimes jumping in display. Also Burton marshes, Shotwick fields, Woolston (50+ Aug), Sandbach. A few visit Fiddlers Ferry. Hale, etc.

Dunlin. The Mersey's most numerous wader, qualifying international importance with 1.6% of W.European counts; Up to 46,500 Feb/77, mostly on Ince Bank and especially when augmentated with birds from the more exposed Dee in gales, making the Mersey about the 5th British estuary. Up to 8,000 have been on Frodsham sludge-beds and the Weaver estuary in January. Up to 44,000 Feb/77 have been counted on Dee tidal roosts, making it 5th or 6th in British estuaries, with up to 30,000 off Red Rocks on January tides, 3,000 below Heswall-Gayton in July, 5,000 Burton marsh, inland up to 50 at

Sandbach, others on passage at Northwich flashes, Frodsham marsh, Hurleston, Woolston and most meres. Occasionally albinistic birds appear and others have been confused for rarities, even broad-billed sandpiper. Ringing shows most come from Scandinavian and Baltic countries, one recovered at West Kirby 13 days after July ringing in Sweden, another from Murmansk on the Dee, and at Warrington 10 days after in south Norway. Another was recovered in East Greenland 14 days after ringing at Hoylake. Both estuaries are important moulting areas. Russian and Scandinavian dunlin of the longer-billed race *alpina* cross the Pennines in late autumn to moult and winter here, returning annually to the same haunts here, while younger birds first moult on The Wash, then winter here. Shorter-billed Greenland *arctica* and Icelandic *schinzii* pass through this area at the end of July and in August for only a short stay, delaying moult until their journey's end in North Africa. Two ringed wintering in Morocco were recovered on West Kirby shore.

Dunlin have nested occasionally in both estuaries, at the Dee's Burton 1939 and 1942, at the Weaver's Weston Marsh, and the Mersey's Cuerdley 1904-7, but regularly on the East border moors in The Peak, 2nd on Denbigh moors, associated with golden plover as its "parasite" rather than "page". It is as a migrant that the dunlin has given most scope to ringers here, *arctica* ringed visiting the Dee in May/69 being shot in July/69 in East Greenland and another recovered in Moroco. One ringed at Hoylake May/70 was in East Greenland 16 days later. Ringed in Baltic Sweden in July and August, they have been at West Kirby by Nov and Dec. One marked at Thurstaston in February was moulting on the Norfolk Wash in the following August's return migration. See Migration.

Turnstone. These colourful, tortoiseshell, chattering waders are the main attraction to visitors around Hilbre's Laminaria shores. They prompted me to call it "Turnstone Island" for an article in The Times in 1934. Some birds may be seen there every month of the year, mostly autumn-winter, 200-500, over 300 in Aug/52. Alone on the island, I had them approaching and taking bread and biscuit-crumbs since I first knew them. Up to 300 roost at high water on rocky islets in Leasowe Bay and on New Brighton breakwaters, and 200 at night on Bidston Moss fields. Up to 150 feed in New Brighton M.L. when drained, up to 12 at New Ferry old sludge-bed and up to 300 may be found feeding regularly among waders on the stony Mersey shore from Egremont to New Brighton Perch Rock, a few on the more sandy Wirral coast to Hoylake Red Rocks, and the Dee Thurstaston, sometimes displaying in May. Their winter range is shown by one ringed West Kirby May/67, and found at Morocco Sept/67. Others recovered at West Kirby Aug/71 and Sept/72 were marked in Morocco Feb and Sept/71. An Icelandic-ringed bird has been recovered here. A few are seen on inland passage, mostly Aug-Sept, by the Mersey at Ince, Frodsham Marsh, Thelwall, Weaver-Rocksavage, Walton old sludge-bed, Sandbach, Northwich Flashes, etc. Fiddlers Ferry, Albinistic birds at Hoylake-Hilbre 1916 and 1972 returned.

Gulls. The most typical Mersey birds to ferry commutors who know only the three-quaters of a mile of sewage which slides past Birkenhead and Liverpool and comes back on the next tide. Massive winter roosts of mostly 5 species of gull have increased to 142,000 on the upper Mersey estuary and 42,000 on the Dee, and fluctuate at large inland roosts like Rostherne 11-20,000, Doddington 13,750, Lostock Northwich 10,123, Barmere 3,650, Hurleston 13,000, Hinckley SQ 2,800, Chelford 5,000, Radnor, Northwich, Farmwood, Tatton, etc, since the food-resource of increasing rubbish-tips increased their breeding stocks elsewhere. Flight-lines to and from these roosts become a characteristic sight towards dusk and sunrise on the Mersey and overland. Of 16 Cheshire spp, 12 are now regularly on the Mersey where 50 years ago I found only 6. A phenomenal increase in little gulls brings up to 450 to the Mersey mouth in spring and autumn passage, and lesser numbers to Hilbre, Weaver, inland to Marbury, etc. Many in immature plumage were missed in prewar's lack of efficient field-guides. Since first appearing in the Irish Sea 1956, Liverpool Bay July/64 and the Mersey 1967, the Mediterranean gull has become a regular sight in lesser numbers, also occasionally inland. Since their nesting extended to North Wales 1920s, great blackbacks may be seen on the Mersey at all seasons and inland in winter. More lesser blackbacks now overwinter when Sabine's has increased, especially in Sept-Oct storms on the coast and estuaries, with a surprise visitor to the Mersey June/86.

New Brighton's old Iceland gull in flight over the Mersey.
(Photo A. Copleston and K. Horton)

There is a marked spring (February) passage of common gulls on the Mersey at Stanlow and the Narrows. Since I saw (and recorded) the first glaucous at Carrington Moss in autumn 1937, this big, aggressive arctic gull has become a regular winter visitor, with up to 8 on the Mersey on passage one February day 1985. In lesser numbers the Iceland, and both inland at tips or roosts. Since first recorded in the Irish Sea in 1822 with 17 prewar records, 6 in the N.W., Sabine's gull has increased as a winter visitor, especially in storms, with 57 recorded at 14 coastal sites, including the Weaver, 1962-84. Some may have been duplicated. About 18 were in the East Irish Sea Sept-Oct 1980. In June 1976, I deposited in Liverpool Museum the skin of an adult female Sabine's gull found dying that month in the Weaver Estuary, with a heavy infestation of tapeworms and flukes, though her ovary-follicles had started to develop. This arctic gull was first recorded on the Dee in 1884.

The world's oldest known Iceland Gull which visited New Brighton shore for 30 years. Liverpool Liver Building in the distance across the Mersey.
(Photo A. Copleston and K. Horton)

The great increase of breeding ring-billed gulls at Toronto, etc, presumably contributed to their appearance on the Mersey and Wirral coasts in 1982-5, and from North America's increase we have also seen laughing and Bonaparte's reach the Dee-mouth, with the Weaver Franklin's in recent years. But the arctic ivory gull has not repeated its claimed 1925 visit to the Mersey. Yellow-legged herring-gulls are seen occasionally, lesser blackbacks sometimes with pink legs and gulls are often stained with oil to the confusion of their watchers. Kittiwakes have increased both as immatures in the Mersey in autumn, and adults alongshore in autumn storms, since their increased breeding stocks around the Irish Sea cliffs. The monumental *Handbook of Birds of the Western Palearctic* has no evidence of the age reached by the Iceland gull. One returned for 30 consecutive winters to New Brighton shore Magazine Lane sewer, until we looked in vain for it in 1985-86. It was never ringed.

Sabine's Gull flying over the Mersey at Seacombe.
(Photo A. Copleston and K. Horton)

Less favourable is the breeding position of gulls. Cheshire's traditional "peewit-gull", the blackheaded, ended its old Delamere colony at Abbots Moss, Newchurch Common (Sandiway) with increasing disturbance and from Oakmere with speed-boating. Some 60-100 attempt nesting at Woolston,and odd pairs have nested at times at Longdendale, Fourways SQ,(Delamere), Frodsham Marsh, etc. The birdless herring-gull nest with eggs claimed at Hilbre in 1945 was brought by boys from North Wales as a prank. Gulls may be seen flying on the Mersey all night at high water, when, disturbed from their roosts on the banks, they often call over town. Most of them feed at sewer-outfalls and Seacombe is a good watching point, as ebb begins. M.N.A. helped a local study of their dissemination of bovine tapeworms.

Terns. Large autumn shoals of sprats entering the Mersey make Liverpool Bay with its shallow mud-sand banks a major feeding ground for migrant terns with their creaking cries — 2,000 in September, the Dee with slightly less, 1,500 in August counts, mostly common, arctic, over 100 little in the Dee mouth early in autumn and over 500 Sandwiches, some visiting Dee steel-pools and occasionally fly-catching; a few roseates which I first recorded off Hoylake July/39 and which have gone so far up the Mersey as Eastham. Ringing shows Northumberland and Norway birds too. Some follow the Mersey ferries in dipping flight, especially in autumn, and upriver to 200 at Stanlow, also the Weaver and up the Dee to the Welsh steelworks pools which have Britain's largest raft-colony of common terns. All occur inland, chiefly after storms, 160 commons at Marbury May/74; 21 Sandbach after NW wind 1/May/83. Forster's tern briefly visited Hoylake from the Welsh Dee's Point of Air Aug/84, a royal off Hilbre Sept/74, the huge Caspian at Marbury and Northwich July/67 and Woodside Sept/75, whiskered at Redesmere Sept/74, Dee steel-pools July/76, Rostherne Sept/69, Frodsham June/70 and plunge-diving Seacombe Sept/70, and gull-billed Hoylake Aug/76, Beach Road end July/82, Hilbre Oct/82, New Ferry Aug/78. An "Aleutian" tern was claimed at Hoylake 1984. Forster's visited the Mersey mouth March/87.

Black terns are regular spring and autumn passage-migrants at most inland waters, especially after east winds and, changing their habits in autumn to offshore seas, visit the Weaver, Mersey from Stanlow (so late as November/67) to Seacombe, the Rock Channel, Hilbre etc, returning to the Mersey to roost at night. Also in the Dee estuary Denhall-Hoylake and Chester Flats and occasionally in the estuaries in spring. The Mersey had 31 from Seacombe to New Ferry Sept/76 and up to 40 August/75; 20 were at Red Rocks by the Dee Aug/75. From 1970-81 20 white-winged black terns were noted, at Frodsham, Weaver, Seacombe, Woodside, Dee steel-pools, Sandbach, Denhall and Doddington, mostly August-October, 2 in May and 3 in June.

Collared Dove. The greatest success story of modern bird-colonisation, breeding all months of the year despite complaints of its illiterate voice. An immigrant from the Low Countries, it has a W. passage April-May along the Wirral coast, Hilbre, Red Rocks, and the Bar Light, Liverpool Bay. First definite record was at Clatterbridge in Wirral 4 June/1959. Next year birds appeared at Haddon Wood, Ness, Sandymoor, Moore, Grappenhall (Warrington), Caldy and Nantwich. It first nested at Wallasey Mariners' Home, 1961. It colonised urban Wirral much sooner than rural south and central Cheshire. By 1964, small colonies were established at the Mariners' Home, Wallasey, Birkenhead, Meols, Ness, Ellesmere Port old flourmills, Stanlow, Bebington, Chester, Altrincham, Sale and Hale. Numbers doubled in 1968 and by 1969 flocks of over 400 were counted at Ellesmere Port and along the Stanlow Causeway-Manisty shrubberries. In recent years, a recession in numbers to their climax fauna at Stanlow-Manisty saw return of more breeding woodpigeons and winter flocks up to 300 clapping out of the trees and feeding on the marsh. A dusky aberration was at Moreton Lingholm Feb/86. The recent decline at Stanlow-Manisty has been replaced by former woodpigeons, as the collared dove settled down to its climax fauna. In Aug/86 I found no collared doves nesting there but woodpigeons back in strength. An albino was at Ince Bank in 1963. Ringing showed influx here from Belgium, Holland, Denmark and Germany and young Cheshire birds dispersing to Solway, West Scotland and all parts of Ireland. A post-juvenile ringed at Ellesmere Port March/68 was recovered at Bremerhaven, Germany Dec/69.

In post-war years, feral pigeons from blitzed Birkenhead-Liverpool docks made daily flight-lines to feed in fields around Ellesmere Port-Willaston and present flocks from derelict flour-mills at "the port" feed on Stanlow marsh. Mediaeval dovecotes exist at Gayton Hall (1663) and Puddington Old Hall. Turtle-doves have declined as summer visitors in old haunts like Haddon Wood (Ness) and Moss-Side, but remain widerspread in the S.W. Stockdoves nest widespread in southern parks like Combermere and flocks of 300 visit Frodsham Marsh, over 30 Stanlow Manisty shore and more on the Dee; 200 at Bagmere, etc, in winter. Escape aviary barbary and Indian turtle-doves occur.

Short-eared and Barn-Owls. The night-shift of owls working in silence fascinates most bird-watchers; but the estuary marshes in particular afford easy daytime views of several short-eared owls hunting together, flying phantoms on long, brown, slowly flapping wings, which scruntinize us with their staring yellow eyes as their flat faces turn towards us. Numbers are related to available rodents and rubbish-tips, August or September to April. Up to 18 have hunted Frodsham Marsh 1980-1, Moss-Side-Walton old sludge below Moore, Leasowe-Meols where they roost in the old market-gardens sheltered by high privet-hedges. Even back in Feb/61, 6 hunted the reeds below Neston sewage-works. Dee high tides bring up to 7 hunting rats flooded from the Spartina beds below Parkgate and Gayton Cottage-Lane, or nearby fields. Odd ones hunt Hoylake golf-links and Red Rocks marsh, they have been seen flying across the Dee from North Wales to West Kirby marsh and hunting voles on middle Hilbre. Up to 3 hunt Manisty Bay Spartina on the Mersey, and regularly visit Woolston, occasionally Northwich flashes. A tawny was once pair-hunting with a short-eared on Frodsham marsh. During vole-plagues, before the Gowy water-table was lowered, pairs occasionally nested between Ince Hall and Thornton-le-Moors. Odd pairs still nest on border moors on the East, Goldsitch, Goyt, etc. Several local dunlin-rings were found in Meols-

The Barn-Owl, taking a rat into a nest-box. Its great decline is one of the great losses in Cheshire birdlife. (Photo Dennis Green)

Moreton pellets, the head of a redwing and a weasel-skull in others; voles and skylarks in pellets at a Hoylake tip. It occasionally nests up the Dane Valley, at Gradbach and Lady Bower Forest above the Macclesfield border. A 1985-6 survey of hundreds of food-pellets of winter short-eared owls on Merseyside revealed 92% field-voles, 5% wood mice, 2% common shrews, plus bank-vole, small birds, grasshopper, dor-beetle, etc.

Spooky moans of tawnies, our commonest owls, break the silence of many suburban trees as well as rural woods. Local rings from blue tits, song thrush and blackbird are recovered in their pellets and prey up to jay and magpie are taken at Burton Mere Wood, etc. The grey phase was at Ince, 1958. Long-eared owls, sometimes seen roosting in winter in woods at Moss-Side, Sandbach Foden's and Burton, formerly nesting at Bidston, Arrowe Park, Irby pines, and eastern pine-plantations, declined to become our rarest breeding owl, with possibly winter visitors. One at Stockport was ringed by friends at a

Formby Mass, West Lancashire, nest and a barn-owlet travelled north from near Northwich to Lytham in the Ribble estuary.

The moon-faced barn-owl is seldom seen sallying forth in ghostly white for its nightly meal of mice, though nesting until recently on the edge of Wallasey (Poulton Road garage), Puddington, Ince Marsh "magazine", Willaston, Runcord, Moore, Greasby, Sandbach, Moss Side and long ago in Chester Cathedral. In 1929, a friend started the first nest-box scheme, successfully breeding from 2 pairs in his Bidston orchard. When I organised the R.S.P.B.'s 1932 breeding census for this area, 239 pairs were noted in Cheshire, 9 in Wirral. The Hawk Trust's 1984 census found this had declined to one of the lowest in the country, 12 pairs from beneath Bidston Motorway Flyover (one bird killed) to Middlewich Ravenscroft. In both censuses most were on the eastern borders. A post-war decline of 85-95% was due to lack of rodent-rich hunting grounds, and suitable nest-sites. Unfortunately, the RSPB never preserved the 1932 records and I am the only survivor who helped in that census traced by the recent census — organiser. A pair reared young on a farm at Rowton near Chester 1986.

The little owl sits in wise meditation on many a post awaiting dusk before hunting, nesting from the Dee steelworks and Eastham to the Ship Canal rockface at Ince, and upper Goyt moors. One ringed at Moore crossed the Mersey to 10 miles NE, near industrial St Helens. In 1959, I ringed and released in a wood on Ince Marsh below Helsby a Scops owl which landed on a ship making for Liverpool. One was shot at Farndon-on-Dee 1868. Little owl nests at Greasby, the Mancot area of Chester, and Clatterbridge.

Sand-Martin. Extraction of mid and east Cheshire's glacial sand provides several colonies varying in numbers annually and often quick to expoit new exposures, chiefly at Sandiway-Newchurch Common, Oakmere, Mouldsworth and Long Ridge (Delamere), Chelford, Lower Withington, Sandmere, Prestbury A 538, the sand-quarries of Arclid, Astbury, Acre Nook, Petty Pool, Tytherington, Prestbury, Nether Alderly; Bent Farm, Wall Hill and Eaton, Congleton, and Hog's Back Lane Quarry Delamere. Several sites lost at Chelford sand-quarry 1986, and Norley Bank where I saw several nesting in 1968. Small numbers nest occasionally in the Ship Canal banks near Latchford-Woolston and Glazebury, the Rivers Dane (Swettenham) and Bollin, and near Chester, etc. Early migrants appear over the meres at the end of March and the last in October, the largest congregations with east winds. Such was their decline from losses in the south Saharan drought in their winter quarters in 1983-4 that a friend in 1984 ringed only 204 adults and 64 young at 7 mid-Cheshire colonies compared with 419 and 500 respectively in 1983. It nests by the River Bollin at Castle Mill and Prestbury, and at Adlington. (River Dean), Sandbach (River Wheelock). 64 nest-holes were at Fiddler's Ferry Power Station lagoons, May/87.

Migration and pre-migration dispersal roosts form at the Dee steel-pools with current year's dispersal young from Shropshire colonies, then show a S.E. emigration through Shropshire-Sussex-France. Sandiway birds emigrated S.E, through Buckinghamshire-Spain, Mouldsworth birds via Norfolk, with a more W return via Somerset (Bristol Channel Severn Valley).

Water-Pipit. Searching bird-watchers have a November-April opportunity to see 12-20 along the Dee marshes, especially at the brook and Old Quay bog below Neston sewage-works until May, Heswall Riverbank Road, Parkgate, and Dee steel-pools, as well as odd visitors to the Weaver, Woolston, Northwich, Sandbach, Sale etc. From October-April 20-100 rock-pipits may winter on the Dee shore below Heswall, Parkgate and Neston and as passage-migrants at Hilbre, New Brighton, Weaver and Stanlow. Tree-pipits are mainly coastal passage-migrants, but nest in declining numbers at Delamere (Hatchmere, Abbots Moss, etc), Peckforton, Alderley Park, formerly at Thurstaston, Helsby-Frodsham hills and Eaton Park. Common squeaky little meadow-pipits nest on Frodsham and Dee marshes etc. and form heavy weather-migrations down the coast in hard spells. The larger Richard's pipit has occurred at Frodsham, Hilbre and the Dee steel-pools and the red-throated pipit at Leasowe fields Oct/84 and Hoylake Red Rocks.

Nightingale. Perpetual poetry boosts its popular appeal; but most public claims are nocturnal robin-song, crepuscular sedge-warblers or twilight song thrushes without the remotest similarity. People who bother to learn its distinctive notes and pauses may hear almost annually a bachelor singing on territory in April or May, as in recent springs in Delamere, Eaton Park, Pulford, Caldy Wirral Way May/80, Sandbach, Barton, Weaverham, etc, and especially in the Bollin and the Dane (Wincle, Macclesfield, etc) valleys. Nesting has never been proved; a claim for one without a singing bird in a Hatherton, Nantwich garden in 1960 lacks adequate evidence. Passage-migrants have been netted and ringed at Bidston Hill (April) and Hilbre (May) and probably move unnoticed through the county unless they stake a song-territory.

Reed-Warbler. Of 23 warblers recorded in Cheshire, the crepusclar reed-warbler is most closely associated with the distributuion of the common reed, increasing with reed-beds in areas like Frodsham and declining with their removal when water-levels were lowered in the 19th century drainage of Wirral's Birket-Fender valley, etc. They are the characteristic crepuscular song in May and June by many meres. The Mersey used to be considered the barrier to further breeding range in the Northwest until the return of large reed-beds at Wigan and Silverdale. It was formerly abundant in undrained Wirral marshes when old Stanlow Abbey had a monopoly of thatching with the abundant reeds of the Gowy and other valleys. Then it died out with the reduction of reeds. From April-October, Rostherne is its major haunt, with surprisingly few if any sedge-warblers; also Tabley, Cholmondeley, Barmere, Tatton Knutsford Moor, Redesmere, Combermere, Northwich Flashes-Plumley, Dee steel-pools, occasionally Bidston Moss, Moreton Carr Lane brickpits, Frodsham Marsh-Weaver, Rock-savage, Woolston-Moss-Side-Old quay Walton Sludge, Neston Dee reed-bed, Hoylake Red Rocks marsh, occasionally New Ferry, Rudheath, etc.

The more elusive grasshopper nests at times scattered from Frodsham-Weaver and Moreton, Bidston and the Wirral Way at Caldy, Heswall and Neston, at Lymm and Dee steel-pools and elsewhere. Sedges are the commonest aquatic warblers with rare visits of Cetti's, great reed and aquatic.

Rook. The tradition of a fine summer forecast by rooks building higher than usual is part of the fallacious folk-lore shared with many counties. Defying generations of farmers' May rook-shoots, their loquacious rookeries, loud with quarrelling, guttural voices now continue to decline from tree-felling and the increasing urban overflow from Liverpool and Manchester sprawling over Wirral and north Cheshire, to the loss of their arable feeding fields. By 1984, their Wirral nests had declined to 257 from 320 in MNA's 1964 rookery survey, and 2,000 in the 1931 census I quoted in *The Birds of the Liverpool Area*. Rooks still nest at Arrowe Park, Clatterbridge, Thingwall-Corner (trees felled 1984), Barnston Church, Thornton Hough in Wirral, and at Alsager, Combermere, Alderley Park, Frodsham Castle Park, Hartford, Congleton (Eaton) and other parts. 346 rookeries with 8,824 nests were listed in 1975. Several rural rookeries in the mid-south increased considerably by 1980, whereas others in Wirral declined or became extinct. No more does a flock from Eastham glean winkles on the Mersey shore. Raucous rooks no longer claim their former trees at Burton Manor or Runcorn Town Hall, Chester's Grosvenor Park or Birkenhead Park. Their trees in Bebington's Teehey Road were felled like those before West Kirby Post Office and the Dee at Denna Hall (in the campaign against Dutch elm-disease). The long black skyline of homing Wirral rooks I watched in my youth crossing the Mersey each winter afternoon, after their morning feeding-flight to the rich farmlands of West Lancashire, still straggles back in much reduced numbers. Those likewise from north Cheshire visiting Manchester's Platt Fields in the 1930s dwindled to only a few by the 1970s. In 1840 they nested below Burton Manor, but few nest around Burton now. Major rookeries are at Twemlow Green, Budworth, Arclid Hollow, and Adlington Gibson Wood. I saw 25 nests in a holm-oak at Thornton Hough churchyard 1982. Peers Wood, Gayton; Oakhanger, Crewe; Alderley Park.

Black congregations in winter roost gathered in recent years in woods at Dane Moss, Mottram Head, Dutton, Whitegate Rostherne, Willaston, Capesthorne, Lower Withington, Mollington Park Big

Wood, (with some crossing the Dee from Wales), etc. In MNA's aerial survey of bird-movements, 6 rooks were recorded flying N over Wallasey at 800 ft in November, on no known flight-line. We have recorded an occasional pied rook, rooks burying acorns, peanuts and pinecones, quenching their thirst with ice, and scavanging urban rubbish-tips for the bits of eggshell, bacon-rind, cinders, oats, currants, meat and gristle I've found as well as earthworms in their urban crops. At Moore, they share the heronry Green Wood and disturb its herons. Longbows were still being made at Warrington in 1890 for rook-shooting. A rook ringed at Spurn (Humber) in November was recorded in Cheshire in February. Rooks still nest at "Rookery Farm" Middlewich.

A female kestrel, a familiar falcon hovering by Cheshire motorways and nesting in towns. (Photo A. Coplestone and K. Horton)

Migration Through Cheshire

Since a Duke of Westminster and two guests killed 128 snipe in 100 minutes on his artificial snipe-shooting bog at Eaton Hall in November 1899, Cheshire ornithology progressed intelligently. Organised estuarine wader-counts revealed 1,293 snipe on the Dee in December. Ringing revealed Cheshire-bred snipe winter in milder Ireland according to winter's severity, and that our winter visitors from Essex, Holland and the Baltic aren't always faithful to the same haunt-one in Cheshire one winter was found in Spain another.

"Blow the wind southerly" in spring's high pressure, and homing wings bring 35 different summer birds back to breed in Cheshire, or rest awhile restocking their energy-fat while passing through to nest elsewhere. The earliest spring migrants like ring-ouzel and wheatear may by-pass the Wirral coast, crossing Liverpool Bay from Anglesey to Walney Island in Morecambe Bay, as in March/84. It was an exceptional wheatear which reached the coast at Meols at the end of February. March usually brings the first to Burton Cop, like Sandwich terns to Hilbre or an early ring-ouzel to Leasowe Common. Eagerness for the first swallow may mistake a sand-martin cutting the sign of summer over the meres or Woolston sludge-bed. A redstart reached Mollington so early as April 5th and a grasshopper-warbler made Meols by the 6th. After common wheatears come Greenlanders up the coast and inland to Nantwich and Altrincham, in May. More than 50 birds pass this way to escape the rigours of the Arctic winter. When many autumn waders pass south, westerlies bring 13 North Americans. Few other European estuaries can then equal their green refuge on the Dee, which had Britain's biggest count of spotted redshanks.

You can see migration taking place with gannets, shearwaters, skuas and divers in any Sept-Oct onshore gale, by a seawatch at high tide from Hilbre lifeboat-slip, or along the prom from Meols to New Brighton. Or where clouds of slender pintail and droves of teal, wigeon and mallard blacken the glistening grey-green marshes of the Mersey at Stanlow as the incoming tide packs Britain's biggest winter flocks of wildfowl. These decline suddenly as they emigrate in February. Looking up one January morning to the nostalgic sound of geese above me at Sandbach Watch Lane Flash, I saw 50 Russian white fronts etched across the sky on their annual way to their Severn Camlad wintering ground above Welshpool. The Dee Cop was their traditional flight-line to Shropshire, and a few still settle below Shotwick and Puddington. At dusk one March evening, musical, bugle-like contact-calls breaking the silence and keeping together a wide skein of 44 Bewick's swans on their spring passage north alerted us to their white wings suddenly appearing at Marbury, low overhead as they turned NE. The return of harriers and short-eared owls to

Pallas' Warbler, ringed Bidston Hill November 1980. (Photo A. Ormerod)

The ring-billed gull, an increasing Cheshire visitor, on Hoylake shore, July 1982. (Photo A. Copleston and K. Horton)

roost off Parkgate; black terns, little stints and curlew-sandpipers drifted by easterlies to the Weaver or Sandbach in their autumn passage from Europe, long, winking wings of terns dipping behind Mersey ferries and in cold spells the flocking wings of chaffinches, lapwings and chuckling fieldfares moving west all mark migration. Early autumn fills the Dee with screeching Sandwich terns and whistling greenshanks; landfalls of autumn or spring goldcrests bring firecrests to Hilbre and Bidston, once to a Chester garden.

One autumn I looked up on Hilbre to see an osprey fly over, an increasing Cheshire passage-migrant which carried on to Llyn Helyg in North Wales to tarry there fishing for a fortnight. Winter brings traditional field-flocks of golden plover to Ashley, Allostock, Ringway airport and Frodsham, an occasional buzzard to Tatton or Welsh ravens to Burton and Wirral.

Less recorded is the departure of birds. Some 2,000 wigeon left the Mersey from 1815 hours till dusk early one April in a score of successive flights E to SE in a light N to NW wind, previously N-NE. A subsequent wigeon-count was down to 7% of the previous week. A spoonbill which spent a fortnight on Frodsham Marsh was watched at 1600hrs early in August, after roosting on one leg, to preen, fly up, then around in small circles, then increasingly larger and higher circles until a speck in the sky, to depart E. Like a fresh fall of snow, the February passage of common gulls whitens Stanlow Bay. A wheatear was so late as 27 October/62 by the Dee at Gayton, a whitethroat at Woolston Christmas 1984, swifts over the Dee 17 Nov/78, a yellow wagtail at Meols SW Dec/63 and a swallow at Macclesfield Boxing Day 1941. A yearling cuckoo at Delamere, Boxing Day 1897, was made sure, by G.F.Gee, to miss the air-line to Africa by shooting it for his collection. Often we crossed the Ship Canal in a launch to Ince Gorse in sunny March to see, like a living painting, Severn Estuary's white-fronted geese resting on their spring return to Russia.

In July evenings I've stood on the edge of the Dee below Neston when my binoculars revealed a skein of goose-like birds strung across the sunset in hump-backed flight. Closer they come until I can see the piebald plumage and pink bill of the leading bird before they turn east and inland, climbing higher into the gathering dusk. They are shelduck heading for the Peak gap in their moult-migration to Heligoland bight. A small moult-migration of a few Canada geese, distinct from the wandering flocks from Tatton, Tabley or private collections, has been seen over the Mersey on August evenings, probably going to Yorkshire or Inverness. One ringed at the latter moulting ground in the Beauly Firth was recovered at Sandbach. Many great crested grebes moult in autumn in a great flock in Menai Straits off Llanfairfechan and off Stanlow and ringing shows some mute swans from Frodsham and Northwich join the moulting flock at Barrow's Cavendish Dock.

Mist-nets being used by Merseyside Ringing Group to catch winter's flock of finches on the Dee steelworks.
(Photo Eric Hardy)

Swan-upping on the Dee. Catching and ringing mute swans on the Dee marshes.
(Photo Eric Hardy)

One searches the countryside with one's ears as well as eyes in spring. Everything suddenly happens at once. A new song is sung almost daily. In 1964, a precocious wheatear reached the Dee Estuary before March and was followed on the 8th by a silent chiffchaff too tired and busy replenishing lost fat to chirp its welcome to authentic spring. A firecrest sang in Bidston Wood, April 1987.

Modern times brought a spring movement of collared doves from Hoylake Red Rocks to the Bar Light and winter is marked by up to 500 bramblings in a swirl of colour as their white rumps rise up with chaffinches, greenfinches, linnets, twites, water-pipits and sometimes rock-pipits beside the Parkgate Boathouse-Gayton shoreside footpath. A marsh-harrier visited Meols Common, Apr/87.

The influence of local contours was shown by an MNA systematic survey in 1955 of the autumn passage of emigrating swallows contracting their front from July until the last on December 4th, through the Bulkeley Gap, between 500 ft Peckforton and Bickerton hills in the SE. Up to 688 were counted a day, sometimes with swifts. Later it was used by chaffinches and common gulls,the latter turning SW along Bickerton Hill to the Dee or Shropshire . A move through the Peckforton-Beeston Gap to the N of this turned SW to join the movement from the Bickerton Gap. SW along Bickerton Hill to the Dee Valley. The emigration flight of moult-migrating shelduck across Wirral to the Weaver is deflected E by Runcorn-Warrington factory-chimneys.

Modern methods take many of the "secrets" out of migration. In the early post-war days of radar we were permitted to use the new Seacombe Tower radar to show much migration takes place far above visibility by watchers on the ground. An MNA survey by aeroplane observations above 500 ft showed lapwings in February heading SSW at 1,800 ft above the Bar Light in Liverpool Bay; dunlin at 600ft over the Mersey in April, at 1715 hrs GMT; and in late October's migration starlings 900 ft over Wallasey, 500 ft over Ellesmere Port, and 2,220 birds over Altrincham heading SE and seen to climb out of a top layer of cloud whose base was 900 ft, top 2,000 ft, in a S wind of 20 knots.

Since 1969 the annual estuarine wader-surveys revealed not only the international ratings of Dee and Mersey, but heavy movements of far northern birds still on passage late in spring: little stints on Dee and Weaver in April, curlew-sandpipers in May, with over 3,000 sanderling and 10,000 dunlin on the Dee in May/72. Also the earlier arrival than books mentioned of autumn passage, with over 20,000 knot, over 4,000 curlew and nearly, 1,000 black-tailed godwits on the Dee in July and 500 sanderlings on West Kirby shore in August.

Sporting literature fostered the fallacy that Britain's major wildfowl-haunts lay far away in the lonely scenic wilderness of

Scottish firths or the privileged country comfort of aristocratic properties of East Anglia's landed gentry. National monthly winter duck-counts, which I began here in 1947, revealed our estuaries led Northwest Europe, increasing threefold since shooting bans on their reserves. Protection from disturbance by Manchester Ship Canal meant more to our winter duck than photogenic scenery replacing the belching chimneys of Ellesmere Port and Western Point, even if the Mersey was an open sewer choked with chemicals and laced with lead.

Ringing has progressed a long way from its original nestling stage, when a young lapwing ringed on the Eastern hills in June 1912 was recovered wintering in Portugal the following November and another ringed near the Cat and Fiddle that July was found in Ireland the following January. We pioneered with clap-nets among Hilbre waders long before its ringing station; but I heard nothing more of nestling meadow-pipits I ringed on Middle Hilbre, or ringed storm-blown gannet and shearwater liberated at Red Rocks. Many people sent me rings they found on dead birds but recoveries were about 2% until mist-nets and Heligoland traps enabled far more adult migrants to be marked.

It has shown the Greenland origin of knot, all in wing-moult here in September and some dunlin; also Icelandic black-tailed godwits with one marked at a Thurstaston field-roost confirming previous distinction by beak-measurements. Spring and autumn ringed plover on the Dee probably migrate between West Africa and West Greenland, the spring birds caught on the Dee putting on weight before leaving. Likewise the Scottish origin of most of our siskins, some moving on to Shropshire, and the Russian (Karelia)-Sweden origin of Mersey and Dee ruffs until recently with two of the three big northern wintering flocks at the Weaver and the Dee steel-pools. I first learned the origin of the Mersey's winter duck in 1932 when Jack Hughes, the last to farm Stanlow Point island before it became a wartime oil-terminal, sent me a Russian ring off a mallard he shot there, and I traced its origin to a nest at Lake Ilmen, Leningrad. Ringing at Hale Decoy has since shown that Mersey teal come from Russian Pechora, Archangel and Karelia, Finland and Baltic Russia. Ringing showed Dee oystercatchers, faithful to their winter quarters here come annually from Faroes, Norway, Shetland, Orkney and the Highlands. Less loyal to the same haunt was a moorhen one winter at Lancashire's Martin Mere, the next near Macclesfield, while a young Danish bird wintered at Sandbach and a Weaver estuary bird headed home via Essex. Ringing showed that tufted duck come from Latvia, Russian Finland and Norway, scoter from Iceland, fieldfares from Finland. A turnstone at West Kirby in May was at Morocco the following September like a Hoylake sanderling. A young Warrington kestrel went to Spain like a Bidston goldfinch and a litte ringed plover at Chelford. Bearded tits visited Wirral and Northwich

Sharp-tailed sand-piper, a rare visitor to the Dee Valley at Weighbridge Road (Puddington-Shotwick) slurryfield October 1973.
(Photo Dennis Green)

Sharp-tailed sand-piper, Weighbridge Road slurry-field. Deeside, Oct 1973.
(Photo Dennis Green)

since the 19th century, before ringing proved Dutch visitors to the Dee's steel pools. Short-eared owls came from Scandinavia to Meols and from Norway to Rocksavage.

Often, however, recoveries are only local, like a ringed mainland little owl I once found dead on Hilbre's tide-line. Nevertheless, they showed that bramblings roosting early in the winter at New Ferry later crossed Wirral to Parkgate shore, Dee steelpools, Burton's roost, Haddon Wood or Frodsham Marsh; that merlins from Moel Fammau in North Wales wintered on Parkgate shore; a few shags from the Isle of Man and Anglesey come to the Dee off Parkgate and Hilbre, and many cormorants from North Wales' Puffin Island and a few from the Farnes inland to the meres. Common terns crossed the north from Farne and Coquet to fish with autumn flocks at the Dee and Mersey estuaries. Dee lapwings went to milder west France as well as Ireland . A magpie flew inland from Bidston to Sale, a Woolston great spotted woodpecker went 40KM N to Blackburn's shopping centre.

Mild from its surrounding estuaries and sea, the Wirral peninsula, the gardener's "God's Croft", is the winter haunt of chaffinches from Scandinavia and Holland, greenfinches from the Midlands and across the Pennines from east Yorkshire, and East Anglia. Redpolls come from Belgium. Reed-buntings come from the Low Countries; some from Humberside and Walney, arrive at field-pits below Heswall in October and stay until spring, excepting when hard weather makes them leave, like one ringed at Woolston and recovered in Somerset and a Devon bird near Manchester. Herons come to Mersey and Dee marshes from colder Midland and Home Countries. Most interesting was an October tree-sparrow from Spurn caught at Willaston in Wirral, though another from Hightown on the south Lancashire coast came to Red Rocks. Park Canada geese cross the Mersey between Liverpool, St Helens and Birkenhead. A Caldy cole tit crossed the Dee to Holywell, blue tits came to Bidston from Bardsey, the Midlands and Lancashire, long-tailed tits from the Midlands to Caldy. A great tit wintering in Delamere returned to Perthshire. Wrens cross the Dee and one marked at Chester in September was in Devon the following January, as surprising as a Bidston robin traced to the Isle of Wight. A hedge-sparrow from Hilbre was recovered 4 years later near Warrington. We could only guess where grey wagtails came from for the winter until an Aberdeen bird was found in January in Arrowe Park. A linnet spending one winter at Burton spent the next in Ireland, probably urged there by harder weather.

Mist-netting and wing and beak measuring showed that two groups of dunlin use the Dee and Mersey marshes, one to winter and moult here, the other on passage to moult in North Africa. The longer-winged and longer-billed northern *alpina* race from NW

Russia, the Baltic and north Scandinavia arrives here from July to September to moult, winter and return March-April, whereas younger birds of this race usually moult on The Wash or in Holland before coming here August-October. The shorter-billed and shorter-winged *arctica* race from East Greenland and *schinzii* from Iceland mostly pass through in May and August, feeding and resting at freshwater pools and delaying moult until winter quarters in Portugal or Morocco. Many dunlin change along the Cheshire, but not to the Welsh, side of the Dee returning annually, and a few move later to Morecambe Bay. A July adult Danish bird was recovered the following December at Bidston. Of course one may also distinguish some geographical races in the field, like white and blue-headed wagtails passing up the Wirral coast in spring and the greyish-brown northern chiffchaff *tristis* we saw at Stanlow Point at the end of November/84, which winters regularly here like undistinguished northern blackcaps, as it is acclimated to colder weather. Likewise the brown and white northern race *acredula* of the willow-warbler, given to me dead from Wallasey Dock Road, 14/1/71.

Speedy recoveries are more indicative of direct journeys than long intervals, e.g. a March goldcrest from Moreton taken 3 days later on a boat off Walney, and a Hilbre bird at the Calf of Man 2 days later. A common tern ringed at Farne July/70 came overland to Hoylake by Aug/70. At 1 a.m. one Hogmanay, a friend mist-netted a little stint at New Ferry shore slurry-bed; by April it was in Holland. A starling from its Aston winter-roost was recovered 9 days later in Baltic Russia, a Deeside oystercatcher a fortnight later in South Uist. An "arctica" dunlin at the Dee steel-pools in May was shot in East Greenland the following July and a swallow ringed there recovered 46 days later at the Congo. Another goldcrest from Heswall one December crossed the Dee to Holywell within a week. A March greenfinch from Wirral was at Blackpool 4 days later. A Frodsham garganey marked in August was recovered in Norfolk in September and a West Kirby knot was recovered a month later at Vendee, in France. Two young bearded tits ringed in Holland Aug/65 were at the Dee steelworks by October. Watchers see such routes, as when a hoopoe was seen coming across the Dee to Red Rocks the day after a friend reported it on the West side of the Great Orme. Then it continued inland across Hoylake golf-course. More local is the spring return of twite to the NE moors. But a chaffinch marked at New Ferry on October puzzled us by appearing in Lothian next month, contrary to its normal winter movement westwards. We picked up a blackbird on Hilbre a fortnight after it was ringed in south Norway.

Bird-watchers soon learn that bird-movements are linked closely to wind-drifts in spring or autumn, and to cold fronts or gales in winter. Cold fronts "push" skylark movements down the coast and some late springs cause reverse movement of NW wheatears before

Migrating curlews, oystercatchers and redshank packing on a December tide 1969 at Hilbre Little Eye. (Photo Dennis Green)

Oystercatchers, redshank and curlew in flight at receding tide, Hilbre Little Eye, December 1969. (Photo Dennis Green)

an advancing cold front. Freezing of the Baltic early in 1979 sent our biggest influx of red-necked grebes, longtail duck, smews and velvet-scoter. When Sept-Oct gales howling across the Irish Sea hit autumn passage of seabirds south, many are "wrecked" along our shores and far inland. Sept/79 blew inshore 957 Leach's petrels, 200 into the Mersey and some 4,000 along NW shores, inland to Sandbach; 4 Sabine's gulls from Hilbre and Meols to the Mersey; 30 arctic, 6 pomerine, 5 great and 3 longtailed skuas off Wirral; 2 great northern divers, 3 Manx shearwaters, and many red-throated divers, fulmars, kittiwakes, shearwaters, gannet and a grey-phalarope — arctic skuas up the Dee to Connah's Quay. Great skuas, kittiwakes and shearwaters have been blown inland to Rostherne, and Britain's only Pacific Kermadoc petrel to Tarporley. An albatross startled a friend at Meols prom in a Sept/78 gale. Kingfishers and little grebes move to the estuaries in winter, and inland stonechats to Hoylake or Meols dunes. Continental bitterns come here.

A daily autumn-winter survey of skylark, lapwing, starling, meadow-pipit and chaffinch crossing the Mersey from Garston Dock on the SE Liverpool shore, showed severe weather increased counts from 75 to a 750 peak in December frost, nearly half heading due S to Eastham—Manisty, and a quarter SE. Larks rose to 350 and lapwings to 450 in January snow. I've been in the slit-trench at Stanlow Point early in a February morning E wind sleet and snow, with redwings coming in so low as to nearly knock me over. A big frost brought 790 coot and 14 species of duck including 5 smew to the Weaver Estuary.

Birds aren't the masters of their own migrations. Wind often drifts them off course. Westerlies which blow North American planes ahead of schedule bring American waders, even rarer passerines, while easterlies brought black terns to the Weaver, a Kentish plover to Frodsham marsh in Aug/82 (though one returned annually for 5 years to the Dee mouth), marsh-harriers to Dee and Woolston and rough-legged buzzards to Wirral. Most interesting was an Asiatic desert-warbler we watched at Meols caravan-camp in Nov/79 coinciding with dust from the Sahara blown at 50 mph in 2½ days, curving out over the Atlantic to reach NW England and Ireland, as if the same wind brought this visitor.

Ringing as well as watching reveals post-nesting dispersal before true migration, like sand-martins coming here from Shropshire colonies, young terns from North Wales, and hobbies observed at Burton and Shotwick in autumn. Cheshire barn-owls have dispersed to The Fylde and East Lancashire. Wood-pigeons came here from the Isle of Man and Ribblesdale. Young pied flycatchers marked in North Wales in June visited Wirral in July before emigrating south. A little grebe came from Lincolnshire while young collared doves from Ellesmere Port went south to Germany as well as north to Blackpool.

Unerringly as racing pigeons home to their lofts, ringing shows the annual return of some birds to the same nesting or wintering haunt:, a swift to Runcorn for 6 years, redshank to Bidston 14 years, sanderling to the Dee 13 years. A redwing wintering in the Burton roost in 1958 was retrapped there the following winter. We have seen the same limping old Iceland gull return for 30 years to the Mersey below New Brighton's Magazine Lane, a glaucous gull return to Hilbre for 15 years and one to Thurstaston shore recently, Kentish plover came for 5 years to the Dee by Red Rocks and Lapland buntings to the end of the military fence Burton marshes. White turnstones and oystercatchers in successive years marked Hilbre flocks, like partly white ruff and house-martin returning on successive autumn passages to the Weaver. Sometimes birds are seen out of season, like a Sabine's gull on the Weaver in June/76, eventually recovered dying. A PM I had conducted on it revealed a load of flukeworms exhausting its food, probably causing the lack of hormone to migrate. However, an immature was also at Seacombe. Some autumn migrants overwinter, like odd green sandpipers up the Weaver Valley and common sandpipers by Dee, Weaver and Mersey.

Many post-nesting birds form autumn roosts, and winter visitors larger ones, partly for shelter from cold nights and better protection from predators, also for hungry, underweight birds like starlings to learn of better, new feeding grounds by following better-fed heavier birds. Vast roosts have been formed by starlings at Stanlow Point, Chester Zoo and the Dee steelworks , Runcorn Bridge, Cammel Lairds at Birkenhead Docks, Knutsford, Huntingdon, Rostherne reeds and Willaston. Long-eared owls made small roosts at Sandbach Fodens' Flash, Moss-Side, Moreton, Frodsham and Burton Point, Wirral; pied wagtails cross the Mersey to winter roosts in Liverpool's India Buildings and in reeds at Woolston, Knutsford Moor and Lindow Common, while grey wagtails roost singly as behind Birkenhead Hamilton Square. Cormorants roost at high tide on the Dee banks below Neston and inland at Rostherne Mere (with visitors from south Lancashire flashes). Bramblings roost below New Ferry baths, and at Haddon Wood, Eastham, Petty Pool and Cholmondelley. Mersey peregrines have roosted singly on Ellesmere Port's gasometer, Woodside ventilator and Liverpool's Metro and Clarence Dock Towers; Dee peregrines on the Dee steelworks gasometer and Connah's Quay power-station. Harriers roost on the marsh off Parkgate and short-eared owls at Meols old market-gardens. Up to 20,000 wood-pigeons roosted at Sandbach Fodens' and Mottram Hall.

Most colourful is the roost of northern golden plovers as they assume spring plumage on Frodsham No 1 sludgebed. Local corn-buntings form small roosts at Woolston and Knutsford Moor, migratory redwings at Woolston and other woods while high tide roosts are formed by Dee waders at Hilbre, West Kirby shore,

Thurstaston, Denhall, Mersey birds at Ince and New Ferry and at very high tides on Frodsham Marsh. Ringers showed the rhododenron-roost on the Common side of Burton Wood was used by chaffinches and bramblings from the Low Countries, redwings from Norway, blackbirds from Sweden, greenfinches from Wirral, Scandinavia and the Midlands, song thrushes from North Wales. They showed the Dee steelworks reed-bed swallow-roost, peaking at 25,000 early in September, had birds from Northern Ireland, Yorkshire and Staffordshire. Most came from 30 miles radius, some interchanging with roosts at Knutsford, Lower Withington and Macclesfield. One marked at Shotton was at Sandbach next day. They showed these swallows avoid the Welsh mountains and coast when they emigrate SE over Shropshire to Essex, Kent and Sussex. A Gloucestershire recovery showed some return by the Severn Valley route. Most use the same route annually on a broad front day or night via Spain, Algeria, West Cameroons (October) and Nigeria (November) to winter in South Africa (December-April). Swallows also roost in New Ferry shore-reeds below the baths, gathering over the nearby Mersey. A greenfinch ringed at the Dee steelworks was recovered in Surrey, 165 miles south, released and recovered back at Chester near its origin.

All bird-watchers and especially duck-counters are confused by exotic duck which I consider guilty of escaping from collections unless, like ruddy duck, they establish self-generating wild colonies. All hybrid ducks and geese I discard as escapes. Aviary escapes range from choughs (formerly free-flying pets at Barnston) to even budgerigars confused for bee-eaters. One local Cheshire Bird-Report included an immigrant humming-bird hawk-moth as an escaped "humming bird". Cheshire falconers keep golden eagles, peregrines, gyr, goshawk, lesser kestrel, merlin, red kite, buzzard, even eagle-owl. While 50-80% of trained hawks and falcons are eventually lost or deliberately hacked back to the wild, aviary-bred birds like sparrow-hawks, kestrels, etc, are liberated, and others like tawny eagle, red kite, etc, have escaped.

Even in suburban areas, winter siskins visited a Temple Avenue, Birkenhead bird-table and waxings a Mendip Road garden. A pied wagtail roost was in Grange Road, 1972. Long-eared owl and pied flycatcher visited a Wallasey, Liscard garden where a grey wagtail roosted in the shopping centre. A grey wagtail roosted in Chester Abbey Square, black redstarts nested off City Road, 1973 and spotted flycatchers at the cathedral. Birds are sometimes dyed with unnatural colours to observe their movements, like Mersey duck yellow above and below the tail. A lesser black backed gull dyed on its neck when feeding in the nesting season at a Leigh, south Lancashire tip, was next seen feeding at Bidston tip, the furthest of birds traced back to the big colony on Walney Island in north Morecambe Bay. Yellow-dyed dunlin from The Wash and wing-tagged redshank from the Ribble are further observations while dunlin dyed on the Dee were loyal to their respective Welsh/English side. Wintering blackcaps and chiffchaff may come from N. Europe.

Inevitably, we come back to the search for a new bird for one's life list — the black-throated thrush at Sale golf-course in Nov/83, a golden oriole in Thame Valley at Denton May/83, a red-breasted flycatcher in a Doddington garden Sept/78, a bluethroat near Macclesfield, May/80, and a November yellow-browed warbler in Bramhall Park — Cheshire can produce them for the "twitchers".

Migration times vary with wind-direction chiefly; but seasonal expectations are a fair guide to the bird-watcher who isn't on the end of the grape-vine telephone. Here are a few of many monthly opportunities

January. The young year, usually colder, may bring big weather-movements of skylarks to the Dee in frosts. Twite reach a peak there with an occasional Lapland bunting. A dozen different duck, including over 500 pochard have been at Rostherne. Mersey wigeon

Cheshire's first stilt-sandpiper which spent much of 1984 on a Frodsham Marsh field, and at Northwich. (Photo A. Copleston and K. Horton)

and mallard often peak. Smew and longtailed duck are likely on north Cheshire meres and in hard weather very large flocks of lapwings move westwards, little grebes and duck reach their best on the Weaver Estuary, and bramblings among finches flocking on Parkgate-Gayton shore or Stanlow thickets. In 1982 a blue tit fed on frozen Manisty shore. Over 1,000 black-tailed godwits are sometimes on the Dee marshes opposite Burton, but it was mild enough for a late wood-sandpiper at the steel-pools in 1973, a spotted redshank elsewhere and in 1985 two comman sandpipers and little stints at the Weaver. However, a slavonian grebe was also off Parkgate. Firecrests may be among the goldcrests, while at dusk odd woodcock roosting in Haddon wood flight down to the Dee marshes at dusk. A winter influx of reed-buntings from the Midlands, sometimes continental visitors augments roost of 200 at the Dee steelworks. Over-wintering green sandpipers may be at Norbury, Hurleston and the Weaver. Blackcock "lek" near the road at Swallow Moss on the Staffs. border. Cold weather brings winter movements of blackcaps coastwise to milder North Wales from inland, possible North Europe.

A regular transatlantic "drift" migrant, an American pectoral sandpiper, showing white outer tail-feathers, ringed at Halton Moss, Oct. 1960, by Merseyside Ringing Group. (Photo C. Ellis)

A black-tailed godwit, a regular Icelandic bird ringed on the Dee marshes by Merseyside Ringing Group. (Photo C. Ellis)

Unless disturbed by boating, Doddington has its major flocks of shoveler and goosander. Peak numbers of divers shelter from gales at Hilbre. Many gardens have a blackcap left over from summer. An early woodpigeon egg hatched at Mollington on the 31st in 1970 while farmers were still shooting the grey winter flocks. The latest Cheshire yellow wagtail was by the Weaver on the 4th, 1984. A few white fronted geese sometimes drop to fields below Puddington, brent at Tansky Rocks in the Dee month and Bewick's swans on flooded Aldford meadows, Frodsham Marsh and Ince Bank. We counted 166 kittiwakes in a 1981 Hilbre gale. At dusk, thousands of black-headed and herring gulls gather in impressive roost at Rostherne and Tatton, with common gulls at Audenshaw reservoir and mostly blackheads at Doddington. In 1986, the snow-white wilderness left by the blizzard over moor and mossland stretching east to The Peak sent its day-hunting short-eared owls westwards, in a wide influx to hunt our estuaries. On the Dee and at Frodsham, at Meols and Manisty, they turn their cat-like faces directly to one in comic curiosity, gazing with prying yellow eyes as they flap slowly by.

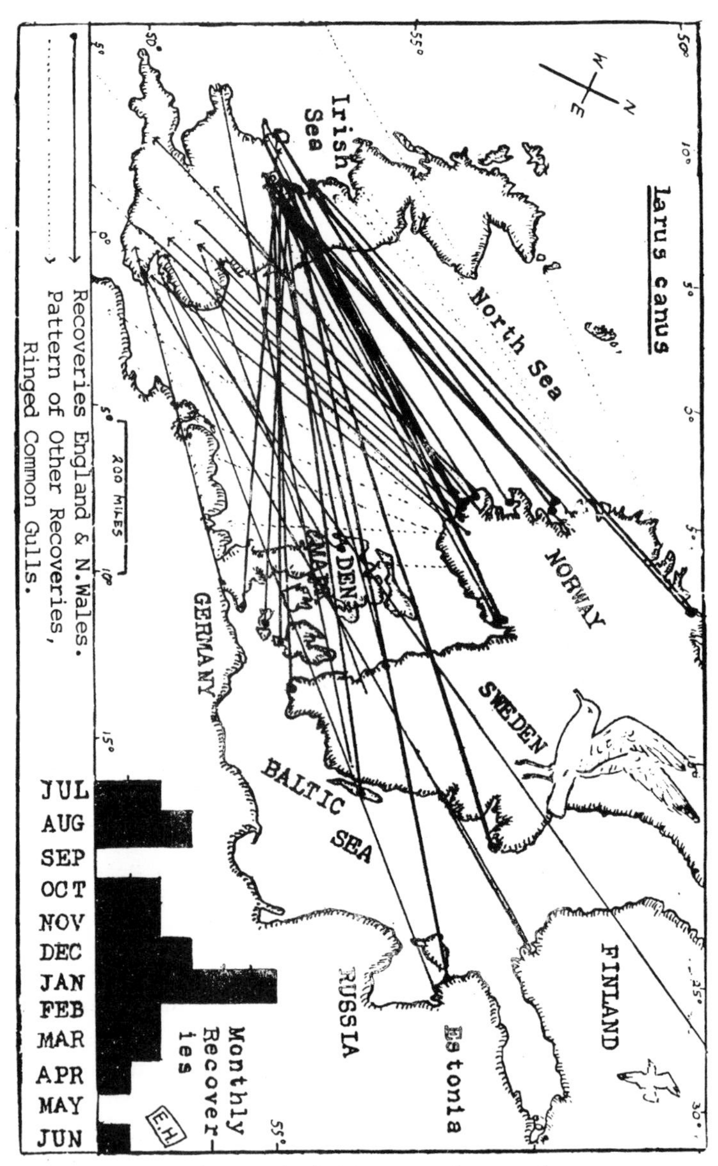

Ringing recoveries showing the Baltic nesting haunts of most common gulls wintering in Cheshire or on passage-migration.

February. In hard frost wildfowl crowd Rostherne Mere below the churchyard, too deep to freeze. Even in cold spells like 1969's raw nor'easter, emigration makes a noticeable decline in the Mersey's big flocks of pintail and teal; yet in mild 1973, 10,395 teal were counted among 23,000 duck early in the month. February has also brought peaks in pintail, dunlin and redshank there and with dunlin, redshank and teal at Sandbach. Great crested grebes returning from the sea flock on Great Budworth and other meres; 2,000 bramblings were at Frodsham in 1976, 50 to 100 goosanders at Doddington with no boats to disturb them. Towards the end, the first collared doves and mistle-thrushes are on eggs. Over 10,000 lapwings flocked by the Dee in 1973. In the "record" Lapland bunting winter of 1956, a party of 30 were on Frodsham Marsh. An early common tern was at New Brighton 1974. After the coldest February for 20 years, February 1986, a record of 6 velvet-scoter visited Rostherne Mere on their way west, and a record 2,100 pochard were counted with over 1,000 tufted duck and 150 ruddy duck.

March. Wild weather stumbling its way to the kindly days of spring brings the first little ringed plover, back by the 9th in 1977 to Sandbach Elton flash and Frodsham, Bewick's swans and some whoopers to Dee, and Mersey, the first screeching Sandwich tern and silent wheatear to Hilbre or the Dee, an early sand-martin skimming a sheltered corner of the meres though only exceptionally an early swallow at the end of the month. The first garganey may appear at Moss Side or Frodsham, the first chanting chiffchaff in Dibbinsdale. A yellow wagtail once reached Tatton by the 26th. The spring passage is noticed in increased numbers of little gulls, mostly juveniles, in Liverpool Bay and the Mersey mouth, golden plover at Frodsham, goldeneye on the meres and scaup off Caldy. Meadow-pipits sing over territory on Frodsham Marsh, Rooks and herons have their first eggs and a tawny owl nest had c/2 at Ledsham on the 13th. White wagtails on passage from S.W. Europe are up the coast and inland to Sandbach, Prestbury sewage-farm and Macclesfield's Wildboarclough and Shutlin's Low, while curlew bubble on territory in Tatton Park. A kestrel was flying past the NW Buoy, Liverpool Bay March/77. I found an early whimbrel at Hoylake 8 March 1941, while 3,000 common gulls marked the spring passage to Scandinavia in Manisty Bay 1983. An early tree-pipit reached Hilbre 29 March, 1981 and its earliest swallow on 13 March 1986, with early whimbrel Hoylake Red Rocks on the 12th and a red-spotted bluethroat there on the 25th.

April. After some false starts, April resurrects spring with days of discovery among the migrants. Southerly swallow-winds bring the first fall of summer migrants along their westerly flyway, led by different early birds some years — wheatears, yellow wagtails or chiffchaffs. Early in the month a ring-ouzel may be seen on Leasowe Common or Hilbre, white wagtails are in the estuary and an early common tern may join the Sandwiches off Red Rock's high tides. Migrating pied flycatchers may rest on hills at Runcorn and Helsby; 75 tree-pipits were counted one morning on Hilbre. On another I watched a migrant goldcrest feeding on seaweed-flies below me. A cuckoo was on Deeside and a black tern at Marbury by the 3rd, a grasshopper-warbler on the 6th, and a ring-ouzel back at its nesting haunts on Shutlin's Low on the 3rd. Marsh-harriers and reed-warblers appear at meres, or Woolston; an avocet has sometimes appeared by Dee, Marbury or Weaver and, less common than in autumn, wood-sandpiper at Sandbach, an early black tern at the Weaver and rarer still a Leach's petrel off Leasowe, 1984. The first whimbrel's repetitive whistle is heard over Dee and Mersey, little gulls visit Hilbre and garganey regularly visit Denhall and Weaver pools. Spring-passage is shown also with increased numbers of purple sandpipers on Hilbre and if April and May are dry, and water-levels are lowered at flashes and meres, unusual numbers of godwits, dunlin, turnstone, ruff, wood-sandpiper, sanderling, grey plover, little and common ringed plovers, spotted redshank and other waders are seen inland. Suddenly people start eyeing lakes for the flash of the first swallow and mistake an earlier sandmartin. At the end of April the first migrating swifts on sickle wings scurry across the wide-stretching sky in their wild career.

Northern golden plover, 1,650 one day, assume magnificent nuptial plumage in the fields below Frodsham and Shotwick. Kingfishers now take up territory along Bollin, Dane, Dean, the Dee at Eaton and sometimes even Bramhall's Ladybrook. In the Dee estuary and at the meres, watchers are apt to tick a continental record when they see light-headed cormorants, but these are British birds assuming sometimes a grizzly white head-feathering I've often seen in their North Wales colonies. Occasional yellow-legged herring gulls are more reversions to their ancestral form than continental visitors. Returning in a local movement, a wren was crossing Liverpool Bay at the Bar in 1967. A blue-headed (Continental type) yellow wagtail mated with a normal British race at the Dee steelworks June/70, and a pair at Meols in 1954. Dotterel visited Sealand Apr/87.

May. Where woods grow greener, the purring turtle-dove sets the mark of May with final proof of spring; but it's a declining visitor to the west. More whimbrel fill the Dee with tittering calls — 23 below Heswall West Park one day, Green land wheatears follow the earlier common kind up the coast where the spring passage of arctic ringed plover and sanderling marks the tideline. Even dotterel are seen occasionally at Frodsham and Doddington, though less often than on the Welsh tops. More marsh-harriers may include an occasional passing Montagu's at Frodsham, Woolston or the Dee where there were still 17 water-pipits at Neston one year and reed-warblers sing in the reed-bed by the shore. In 1972, easterlies brought Temminck's stint to the Dee steel-pools and in 1970 friends distinguished a whiskered tern at Frodsham as well as a summering drake wigeon. A longtailed duck was still at the Dee pools in 1967 and ruffs by a roadside pool at Hazel Grove in the NE. In 1986's late spring, a Caspian tern visited Hilbre at the end of May when quail were calling at Denhall by the Dee. In 1982 a subalpine warbler was at Wilmslow. There's still the spring passage of little gulls and kittiwakes offshore on high tides and although ring-ouzels are back on their eastern hills in April, late birds heading further north may still be seen, like one at Lower Withington in 1967. I have seen kittiwakes remaining off Meols, as on the Seaforth side of the Mersey. A late spring passage of arctic race of dunlin *tundrae* may be seen on the Dee as at Thurstaston. Up to 9 little gulls were at Marbury in 1975, and 21 Sandwich terns at Sandbach 1983, where a nightingale appeared in 1980. Nightingales have appeared occasionally at Caldy, Dibbinsdale and the East Cheshire cloughs. Curlew nest occasionally near Nantwich and other parts of South Cheshire and there is a May record of a bluethroat in East Cheshire. A firecrest sang in Bidston Wood, brambling at Peckforton 1987 when a red-necked grebe was off Hoylake and a white-winged black tern at Shotwick Lake.

June. The rose-petalled face of summer may bring quail with twitching calls in barley-fields from Heswall to Frodsham and Manley, while 700 mallard flock off Manisty, mostly drakes, before their summer moult. The screeching colony of common terns on the Dee steelworks reserve's raft are feeding young on sprats, sand-eels, sticklebacks and tiny postage-stamp sized flounders, from downriver as Heswall and Hilbre. A passing osprey has sometimes been seen fishing Rostherne, Great Budworth and Farmwood Pool. Little stints, black tern and garganey may be at Sandbach and sometimes, as in 1975, a pair of black-tailed godwits which now nest at the Ribble Estuary north of Cheshire may seek territory by the Weaver, or somewhere undisturbed. Shearwaters, fulmars and kittiwakes appear off Hilbre. A spotted red-shank in summer plumage was still on Ince Bank, 1975, and a greenshank at Parkgate 1974. Cory's shearwater off Hilbre June 1986 coincided with a summer passage of this Atlantic seabird off Cornwall. A raven at Macclesfield Forest 1986.

July. The sun no more "goes north". The tide of migration turns, bringing large flocks of knot and other waders to weekday Dee tidelines below West Kirby; but weekends too often find them disturbed by ignorant or selfish owners of loose dogs along the shore. Little stints, curlew-sandpipers, little ringed plovers and rarer waders are among the Weaver estuary ruffs and up to 600 dunlin. Temminck's stint may be with green and wood-sandpipers at Sandbach, plus a good chance of an American, if only a "pec", on westerlies to start the records of wader-hunting. From Hilbre to Meols this is usually the peak time for kittiwakes, gannets and skuas, chiefly arctic but sometimes longtailed, with onshore winds. Large flights of curlew in impressive fly-pasts mark the tide at Stanlow Point. In July and August, 40/50 greenshank whistle over the Dee marshes and a hobby's bow-shaped wings may mark the sky over

Burton or Shotwick fields. Evening moult-migration flocks of shelduck over the Dee at Neston and Burton or from the Weaver and Runcorn should not be confused with the circling flights of immature shelduck, which return later. Larger gatherings of hundreds of swifts may be seen feeding over the Weaver Bend (1,000 sometimes) Burton marshes, Budworth mere, Rostherne or Tatton. July, August see the first influx of adult dunlin in the estuaries, North Russian birds here to moult and the first young Baltic birds. Up to 100 flightless moulting guillemots may be seen at the Bar Light, and in stormy 1968, 50 Balearic were there with Manx shearwaters and a glaucous gull. Later in the month, mostly common terns begin following Mersey ferries and Sandwiches return to the Dee. In 1972 an unexpected roseate appeared at the Dee steelpools. In 1986 a red-necked phalarope visited the Weaver estuary after an American pectoral sandpiper earlier in July.

August. When almost golden grouse are greeted with gunshot on the moors above Crag Hall, the last golden plover and curlew are disturbed off to the lowland Mersey marshes. Shooting days stimulate emigration. Already counts of 2,700 waders of 16 to 18 species there are mostly 1,000 dunlin, curlew, lapwings and redshanks, with whimbrel and the odd little stint on Ince Bank as well as 300 terns, including occasional Sandwich. Pintail and wigeon appear, and there are already up to 2,250 teal. Off the Mersey-mouth little gulls are flocking and a moulting guillemot may drift in to Seacombe. Purple sandpipers appear at Hilbre and at Hoylake Red Rocks and early "pom" may be among the arctic skuas harassing the terns at high water. On the Dee marshes, curlew-flocks peak in August and September when spotted redshanks come; the first kingfisher appears in the gutters and the first merlin along the shore. Curlew-sandpipers total 11 by the Weaver and may be among waders below Heswall. Black terns appear inland over the meres as well as the Weaver Bend, where ruffs peak, as at Woolston, and swifts still congregate. A sharp-tailed sandpiper was there Aug/83. Ringed plovers, greenshank and green sandpipers peak there until early September; up to 46 curlew-sandpipers have been counted and rarer waders may include red-necked phalarope and annually a pectoral sandpiper. Up to 30 herons now fish there, and a marsh-harrier is to be expected at Frodsham and garganey on the Weaver. In 1970, a little bittern visited Frodsham Marsh; the previous year brought a spotted crake. An osprey visited Sandbach in 1970 and Wilson's phalarope came in 1970. Combermere also had a visiting osprey, while Frodsham pools are now marked by the passage of sedge-warblers. In August 1986, I watched a migrating dotterel by the Dee steelworks marsh 2,800 lapwings at Sandbach Watch Lane Flash while green legs, etc, prompted friends to claim an American least sandpiper with little stint wood-sandpiper and black-tailed godwits at the Dee rifle-pools. A red kite flew over Puddington and a crane spent 3 weeks around the marshes.

September. There's no rest for the wader-hunter, photographer or ringer. Warm, high pressure and easterly winds bring a Continental drift; westerlies bring the Americans. High westerly gales tearing in from the Irish Sea with high tide bring autumn's best migration, blowing their airline onshore. In September 1986 east winds brought a penduline tit to Carr Hall Farm, by Carr Lane brickworks pools Moreton. Avocet, or an American pectoral sandpiper, may be hoped for among the ruffs at Sandbach, occasionally maybe knot or grey plover among unusual inland visitors while the Weaver shows a movement of terns into Cheshire as well as 30 or more ruffs and 40/80 black-tailed godwits. Among Frodsham's Americans, a buff-breasted sandpiper appeared in 1968 and another with a long-billed dowitcher and two "pecs" in 1970. An American Wilson's phalarope was there with a white-rumped sandpiper, pec and buff-breasted in 1981, while flocks of house-martins and swifts are still a feature. Pintail and wigeon begin to mass on Mersey and Dee and the shooting season drives birds on to the reserves. Curlew peak on the Mersey where an arctic skua may pursue terns up to Runcorn. The full moon brings in wigeon from the continent and over 5,000 teal can be counted at high water. Cormorants may well exceed 100 at their Dee high tide roost below Neston if gales have driven them in from Liverpool Bay, gales which bring kittiwakes, gannets, Leach's petrels, grey phalarope, skuas and occasionally a sooty shearwater along the coast from Hilbre to Leasowe and New Brighton. The first winter scaup appear off Caldy, over 30 greenshank may still be below Parkgate. Greenland and Iceland dunlin are on the Dee where mallard reach near 3,000 and up to 17 kestrels may hang in the air searching the steelworks marsh for voles. The steelworks reserve had a bluethroat in 1971. Black tern, up to 13, appear on the Mersey off Seacombe and storms bring the odd Sabine's gull there or off Meols. The first short-eared owls appear gazing with prying yellow eyes from the Dee (with hen-harrier) to Meols and Frodsham. This is the best time to see guillemot and razorbill off Hilbre-at low water in 1968 a wood-sandpiper flew whistling over me. Great crested grebes from the meres are gathering in the Dee-mouth while early this month swallow-roosts reach their peak at the steel-works reserve as well as Woolston, Huntingdon and Knutsford. Up to 36 curlew-sandpipers and 60 ruffs may be with black-tailed godwits, little stints and other waders and shoveler at Woolston. Montagu's harrier visited Sale Meadows in 1971 and an osprey in 1980. Over 100 ruddy duck may be on Combermere, yet on the 2nd in 1984, a yellow hammer was on eggs at Mouldsworth in Delamere.

October. Onshore gales still bring the best chances for seeing shearwaters from Hilbre to Meols, Leach's petrels and grey phalaropes, shag, guillemots, razorbills up the Wirral coast and a Sabine's gull off Seacombe. Sometimes the weather goes wild. A soaking blast of Irish wind lashes the Wirral coast with raging surf, blowing in the autumn passage of seabirds — a record 40 pomerine skuas in Liverpool Bay in 1984 when the Mersey sheltered longtailed skuas, Sabine's and little gulls, grey phalaropes and black terns from New Brighton to Seacombe. Manx shearwater has been blown up the Dee to Queensferry, storm-petrel to Connah's Quay and up the Mersey to Woolston, Leach's petrel to Queensferry and up the Mersey to Stanlow and Ince and gannets to Stanlow (Nov) and Burton. October 1986 brought Woolston Eyes reserve its first ortolan and crossbill in a fall of migrating blackbirds, redwings etc. and in 2 ½ hours in a high tide gale off Moreton promenade 33 Leach's petrels, a storm-petrel and a great skua were counted. Goldeneye appear on West Kirby marine lake and the Weaver when not disturbed by boats. We've had curlew-sandpipers among the waders on the Dee shore. Over 26,000 oystercatchers may flock on the Dee tides, and the main arrival of young dunlin comes from Russia via the Wash. Grey wagtails come down from Scottish hills, even to Meols and Arrowe Park. Water-rails return now and next month to Sandbach and the Dee marshes and black tern may still follow the Mersey ferries. An odd brent goose or two usually appear on the Dee, sometimes up to the steelworks, where a white-winged black tern is sometimes recorded. Golden plover and curlew peak on the Mersey marshes, shelduck on the Dee where 5,000 may mass on the tide off Heswall. The odd firecrest may come with the passage of goldcrests from Hilbre to Bidston, robins may move along the coast and glaucous and Iceland gulls visit Rostherne's winter gull-roost. A kingfisher may come coastwise to Runcorn's Bridgewater Canal, late wheatears may be seen at Burton Cop while Wirral rooks begin their daily winter flights across the Mersey. The motorist may see pochard from roadside Hatchmere, Redesmere and Sandbach Watch Lane. In 1980, Lapland buntings were on Denhall shore and in 1974 we estimated 1,000 common, Sandwich and a few black terns sheltering in Bromborough Dock from a H.W. gale. In 1958 a late red-backed shrike was well seen at Frodsham and in 1971 a tree-pipit was still at Lindow Common on the 31st.

November. Every big weekend tide brings a procession of watchers to Parkgate car-park beyond the Boathouse, not for the peak of Dee dunlin and mallard, but to see hen-harrier, short-eared owl, water-rail, twite, rock-pipit, water-pipit and brambling. Occasionally a few white-fronted geese still drop down, like Bewick's swans, below Puddington and Shotwick, while Shotwick Lake may have a longtail among its diving duck. Rostherne may have its first smew, Tatton its first slavonian grebe, while one or two black redstarts appear on passage to North Wales along the coast at Leasowe or Meols. Arctic skuas are sometimes seen from the Seacombe ferry where I've noticed an occasional flock of scoter fly up-river. Nearly 100 pochard may be on Sandbach Watch Lane Flash and 500 teal with some pintail at Elton (Clay Lane). The Mersey often has its largest wildfowl-counts,with peaks of over 16,000 pintail, mallard, shelduck, wigeon and dunlin. A yellow-browed warbler was in Bramhall Park 1983, Temminck's stint at Frodsham on the 1st 1971, and two roseate terns in the Dee estuary another year on the 2nd. A golden oriole was at Macclesfield on the 2nd 1935 and a wood-sandpiper was still at Altrincham S.F. on the 11th, 1934, In 1979 the desert-warbler still tarried at Meols caravan-camp.

December. The long night month, with waders calling over the marshes beneath the moon, may find a line of Christmas bird-watchers, their numb red noses poking out from a swaddling of mufflers in a savagely cold wind on the tide at Red Rocks corner of the Dee. In contrast, 1984 was mild enough for a spotted crake calling at Sealand aerodrome pool and 1946 for a marsh-harrier to tarry at Thelwall-Woolston-Eyes and 1984 for a whitethroat to be there at Christmas and a common sandpiper at Stanlow. Duck come on the full moon. Continental blackbirds and chaffinches and Scottish song thrushes and siskins are now widespread in Wirral, tufted duck from the Baltic on the Weaver and Moreton flash, and golden plover flocking on Frodsham No. 1 old sludge-field at Saltport. Little gulls, eider and brent may visit Hilbre, pinkfooted geese the Mersey if their Lancashire feeding-fields are overcrowded, or a lone grey crow appear at the tips. Full moon brings further influxes of continental wigeon. Denhall pools on the Dee echo the piping calls of teal, while over 6,000 lapwing haunt the marshes. West Kirby's tide may still reveal 40,000 knot, 200 grey plover and 100 sanderling if loose dogs aren't allowed to flush them to inland fields like Greasby. The Dee may have 17,000 oystercatchers, over 1,000 grey plover off Neston, 20,000 dunlin, while 1,000 black-tailed godwits may roost off Heswall. In 1981, a friend ringed 211 fieldfares in two days, eating windfallen apples in a Daresbury garden. We who are bored by crowded beaches and watch the Mersey winding its polluted way like a greasy serpent from Warrington to New Brighton take pride where industry stands away from its shores and its marshes are left alone to themselves, from Frodsham Score to Manisty Bay — part of the shrinking wild of Cheshire. Crunching one's way through the frozen splendour I saw its sparkling white wilderness after December snow in 1980 darkened by massed wildfowl wings. 53,924 were counted that Christmas, wedge after wedge of wild duck criss-crossing the sky in a confusion of wings while rafts of duck blackened the tide-line. The continental "mealy" redpoll *flammea* visited Bidston Woods 1975, and the arctic race *hornemanni* was at Sandbach Flashes 1972 and the Dee Steelworks. "Twitchers" hurrying around for their 100th "tick" in the year have a wide choice without adding blue-winged teal or an inland barnacle escaped from some duck-zoo. "One of my Baikal teal just flew off this morning", a Delamere friend greeted me when I arrived at his waterfowl-collection. "I'll probably see it in 'British Birds' or the local Bird Report sooner or later!" he added.

A Check-List of Cheshire Birds

Brackets denote scarce or irregular

Nesters: Great crested, black-necked and little grebes; grey heron, mallard, teal, garganey, gadwall, shoveler, tufted duck, (pochard), pintail (1981), ruddy duck, shelduck, (greylag), Canade goose, mute swan, (buzzard), sparrowhawk, (goshawk), (merlin), kestrel, red and black grouse, red-legged and common partridges, (quail), pheasant, (water-rail), moorhen, coot, oyster-catcher, lapwing, common and little ringed plovers, golden plover, snipe, woodcock, curlew, common sandpiper, redshank, (dunlin), (lesser black-backed) and black-headed gulls, common (and arctic) terns, stockdove, feral pigeon, turtle and collared doves, cuckoo, barn, tawny, little, long-eared (and short-eared) owls, (nightjar), swift, kingfisher, green, great and lesser spotted woodpeckers; skylark, swallow, house and sand-martins, carrion-crow, rook, jackdaw, magpie, jay, great, blue, coal, marsh, willow and long-tailed tits, nuthatch, tree-creeper, wren, dipper, mistle and song thrushes, ring-ouzel, blackbird, wheatear, stonechat, whinchat, common (and black) redstart, robin, grasshopper, reed, sedge, garden, willow and wood-warblers; blackcap, common and lesser whitethroats, chiffchaff, goldcrest, spotted and pied flycatchers, hedge-sparrow, meadow, tree (and rock) pipits, pied, grey and yellow wagtails, starling, haw, green, gold, bull and chaffinches, siskin, linnet, twite, redpoll, (crossbill), corn and reed-buntings, yellowhammer, house and tree-sparrows. Bearded Tits have nested at Moore and buzzards at Malpas and Peckforton. Garganey nest in at least three localities.

Winter-Visitors: Black, great northern and red-throated divers, red-necked and slavonian grebes, cormorant, shag, bittern, wigeon, pintail, scaup, goldeneye, long-tailed duck, common, velvet (and surf) scoters, eider, red-breasted merganser, goosander, smew, Russian, Greenland (and lesser) whitefronted, bean, barnacle and pinkfooted geese; dark and light-breasted brents; whooper and Bewick's swans, (white-tailed sea-eagle), (red kite), hen-harrier, peregrine, grey plover, turnstone, black and bar-tailed godwits, knot, purple sandpiper, great black-backed, herring, glaucous, Iceland, common, Mediterranean and little gulls; kittiwake; razor-bill, common (and black) guillemots, little auk, shorelark, raven, hooded crow, (chough), (nutcracker), (bearded tit), fieldfares, redwing, rock and water-pipits, great grey shrike, (serin), waxwing, mealy redpoll, (2-barred crossbill), brambling, Lapland and snow-buntings, puffin.

Passage-Migrants and Stragglers: Fulmar, Manx, Cory's, sooty, little, Maderian and great shearwaters; albatross, storm, Leach's and Kermadoc petrels; gannet, purple and night herons, little bittern, little egret, spoonbill, white stork, glossy ibis, rough-legged buzzard, black kite, honey-buzzard, marsh and Montagu's harriers, osprey,